Certification Study Companion Series

The Apress Certification Study Companion Series offers guidance and hands-on practice to support technical and business professionals who are studying for an exam in the pursuit of an industry certification. Professionals worldwide seek to achieve certifications in order to advance in a career role, reinforce knowledge in a specific discipline, or to apply for or change jobs. This series focuses on the most widely taken certification exams in a given field. It is designed to be user friendly, tracking to topics as they appear in a given exam and work alongside other certification material as professionals prepare for their exam.

More information about this series at `https://link.springer.com/bookseries/17100`.

Certified Kubernetes Administrator Study Companion

Preparing for the Linux Foundation's CKA Exam

Piyush Sachdeva

Apress®

Certified Kubernetes Administrator Study Companion: Preparing for the Linux Foundation's CKA Exam

Piyush Sachdeva
Brampton, ON, Canada

ISBN-13 (pbk): 979-8-8688-1512-6				ISBN-13 (electronic): 979-8-8688-1513-3
https://doi.org/10.1007/979-8-8688-1513-3

Copyright © 2025 by Piyush Sachdeva

This work is subject to copyright. All rights are reserved by the Publisher, whether the whole or part of the material is concerned, specifically the rights of translation, reprinting, reuse of illustrations, recitation, broadcasting, reproduction on microfilms or in any other physical way, and transmission or information storage and retrieval, electronic adaptation, computer software, or by similar or dissimilar methodology now known or hereafter developed.

Trademarked names, logos, and images may appear in this book. Rather than use a trademark symbol with every occurrence of a trademarked name, logo, or image we use the names, logos, and images only in an editorial fashion and to the benefit of the trademark owner, with no intention of infringement of the trademark.

The use in this publication of trade names, trademarks, service marks, and similar terms, even if they are not identified as such, is not to be taken as an expression of opinion as to whether or not they are subject to proprietary rights.

While the advice and information in this book are believed to be true and accurate at the date of publication, neither the authors nor the editors nor the publisher can accept any legal responsibility for any errors or omissions that may be made. The publisher makes no warranty, express or implied, with respect to the material contained herein.

Managing Director, Apress Media LLC: Welmoed Spahr
Acquisitions Editor: Anandadeep Roy
Development Editor: James Markham
Editorial Assistant: Jessica Vakili

Cover designed by eStudioCalamar

Distributed to the book trade worldwide by Springer Science+Business Media New York, 1 New York Plaza, New York, NY 10004. Phone 1-800-SPRINGER, fax (201) 348-4505, e-mail orders-ny@springer-sbm.com, or visit www.springeronline.com. Apress Media, LLC is a Delaware LLC and the sole member (owner) is Springer Science + Business Media Finance Inc (SSBM Finance Inc). SSBM Finance Inc is a **Delaware** corporation.

For information on translations, please e-mail booktranslations@springernature.com; for reprint, paperback, or audio rights, please e-mail bookpermissions@springernature.com.

Apress titles may be purchased in bulk for academic, corporate, or promotional use. eBook versions and licenses are also available for most titles. For more information, reference our Print and eBook Bulk Sales web page at http://www.apress.com/bulk-sales.

Any source code or other supplementary material referenced by the author in this book is available to readers on GitHub. For more detailed information, please visit https://www.apress.com/gp/services/source-code.

If disposing of this product, please recycle the paper

To my pillars of strength—my parents, whose unwavering support and sacrifices have shaped my journey. Your belief in me has been my guiding light through every challenge and triumph.

To Himani, my better half and strongest advocate. Your endless encouragement and steadfast belief in my capabilities have given me the courage to chase my dreams. You make everything possible.

To my brother Lakshya, for being my constant companion and unconditional support in every phase of life.

To my precious bundles of joy—Kashvi and Krishiv. You are my lucky charms who have transformed our lives with your innocent smiles and boundless love. This book is a testament to the inspiration you bring to my life every single day.

This book is a celebration of your love, support, and the beautiful moments we share together. Thank you for being my reason to strive harder and dream bigger.

With love and gratitude,

Piyush Sachdeva

Table of Contents

About the Author xvii

About the Technical Reviewer xix

Acknowledgments xxi

Introduction xxiii

Part I: Kubernetes Fundamentals 1

Chapter 1: Introduction to Kubernetes 3

The Container Management Challenge 3

Container Failures 4

Scale and Complexity 4

Operational Challenges 5

Enter Kubernetes 5

When Not to Use Kubernetes 6

Chapter 2: Kubernetes Architecture 7

Nodes 8

Control Plane vs. Worker Nodes 9

Control Plane Components 9

    API Server 10

    Kube-Scheduler 11

    Controller Manager 12

    ETCD Server 12

    Cloud Controller Manager 13

TABLE OF CONTENTS

Worker Node Components 13
    Kubelet 13
    kube-proxy 14
    Container Runtime 15
Summary..16

Chapter 3: Kubernetes Installation 19

Kubernetes Single-Node Installation Using KinD 20
    Prerequisites 20
    Installation 20
    Kubernetes Multi-node Installation Using KinD 22
    Summary 24

Part II: Workloads and Scheduling 25

Chapter 4: Pods in Kubernetes 27

Imperative Way 28
Declarative Way 29
Pod Lifecycle...30
    Container States in a Pod 31
Inspect the Pods 31
Multi-container Pods...32
Environment Variables in Kubernetes 35
Summary..36

Chapter 5: ReplicaSets, Replication Controller, and Deployments......37

Replication Controller...37
ReplicaSet 38
Deployment 39

viii

TABLE OF CONTENTS

    How to Perform Rolling Updates/Rollback 42

    Summary 44

Chapter 6: Services in Kubernetes 47

    ClusterIP 48

    NodePort 49

    Load Balancer 52

    External Name 54

        Role of Selectors in Service 54

    Summary 55

Chapter 7: Namespaces 57

    Namespace Management 58

    Summary 62

Chapter 8: DaemonSet, CronJob, and Job 65

    DaemonSet 65

    Job 67

    CronJob 68

    Summary 69

Chapter 9: Static Pods and Scheduling 71

    Static Pods 71

    Manual Scheduling 72

    Labels and Selectors 73

    Taints and Tolerations 74

    Node Affinity 76

    Resource Requests and Limits 77

TABLE OF CONTENTS

    configmap and Secrets 79

    Secrets 81

    Summary 83

Chapter 10: Autoscaling in Kubernetes 87

    HPA (Horizontal Pod Autoscaling) 88

    VPA (Vertical Pod Autoscaling) 89

    Metrics Server 90

    Cluster Autoscaling 92

    NAP (Node Auto-provisioning) 93

    Liveness vs. Readiness vs. Startup Probes 93

    Summary 97

Chapter 11: Manifest Management Tools 99

    Helm 99

    Getting Started with Helm 100

    Kustomize 102

    Getting Started with Kustomize 102

    configmap Generator 104

    Managing Multiple Environments 105

    Summary 107

Chapter 12: Authorization and Authentication 109

    Authentication 109

    Authorization 110

    Authorization Types 111

    RBAC (Role-Based Access Control) 112

    Authentication and Authorization in Kubernetes 113

TABLE OF CONTENTS

What is Kubeconfig? 117
Service Account 118
Summary..119

Chapter 13: Network Policies 121
CNI (Container Network Interface) 122
CNI Installation...122
Network Policy Implementation 123
Summary..128
Workloads and Scheduling Review Questions 129

Part III: Storage 131

Chapter 14: Kubernetes Installation Using Kubeadm 133
Prerequisites for Installation 133
Virtual Machine Setup..134
Open the Required Ports for Networking 135
Configure Security Groups 135
Set Up Master Node to Deploy Kubernetes Components.................................137
Validating the Installation...141
Implement and Configure a Highly Available Control Plane 142
High Availability Using Stacked Control Plane 142
    Prerequisites 142
    Load Balancer Configuration 143
    Certificate Management 146
Summary..147

xi

TABLE OF CONTENTS

Chapter 15: Storage in Kubernetes 149

Lifecycle of a Volume and Claim 150

    Static Provisioning 150

    Dynamic Provisioning 150

PersistentVolume 150

PersistentVolumeClaim 151

    Access Modes 152

    Reclaim Policies 152

    Demo Provisioning a Pod with Persistent Storage 153

StorageClass 155

Default StorageClass 157

Summary 159

Storage Review Questions 160

Part IV: Services and Networking 161

Chapter 16: Kubernetes Networking 163

Host Networking 163

Pod Connectivity 164

Container Network Interface (CNI) 165

CoreDNS 166

Troubleshooting DNS Resolution 166

Ingress in Kubernetes 169

    Set Up an Ingress 171

    Ingress Controller Setup 171

    Ingress Resource 171

    Troubleshooting Common Ingress Issues 175

TABLE OF CONTENTS

Gateway API 176

    GatewayClass 176

    Gateway 177

    HTTPRoute 178

    Traffic Flow 179

Summary 179

Chapter 17: Operators and Custom Resources 183

Demo Creating Custom Resources 185

Operators 186

Operator Features 186

Different Ways to Write an Operator 187

Admission Controller 188

Admission Webhooks (Dynamic Admission Controllers) 188

Webook Failure Troubleshooting 192

Summary 193

Services and Networking Review Questions 195

Part V: Cluster Architecture, Installation, and Configuration ... 197

Chapter 18: Cluster Maintenance 199

Node Maintenance 199

Drain Nodes 199

Node Uncordon 200

Summary 200

Chapter 19: Kubernetes Version Upgrade Using Kubeadm 201

Kubernetes Upgrade Process 202

Upgrade Master Node 203

    Upgrade Kubeadm Using the Below Command 203

xiii

TABLE OF CONTENTS

    Verify the Kubeadm Version 203

    Verify the Upgrade Plan 203

    Upgrade CNI Provider Plugin 204

    Drain the Node 204

    Upgrade the kubelet and kubectl 204

    Restart kubelet 204

    Uncordon the Node 204

    Verify the Upgrade on Control Plane Node 205

    Upgrade Worker Node 205

  Summary 205

  Cluster Architecture, Installation, and Configuration Review Questions 206

Part VI: Troubleshooting 207

Chapter 20: Monitoring, Logging, and Alerting 209

  Monitor Cluster Components 209

    Cluster and Node Logging 210

    Debugging Kubernetes Nodes with Crictl 211

  Summary 212

Chapter 21: Troubleshooting Application Failure 215

  ImagePullErrors 215

  CrashLoopBackOff 217

  Pods Stuck in Pending State 218

  Terminated State 220

  Service Not Accessible 222

  Connection Refused Between Pods and Services 223

  Service Selector Mismatch 224

  Summary 225

Chapter 22: Troubleshooting Control Plane Failure 227

API Server Troubleshooting 227

Kubeconfig Troubleshooting 228

Kube-Scheduler Troubleshooting 228

Kube-Controller Manager Troubleshooting 229

Kubelet Troubleshooting 229

Summary 231

Chapter 23: JSONPath 233

Multiple JSONPath Queries to Fetch Details 234

JSONPATH Custom Columns 235

Summary 236

Troubleshooting Review Questions 237

Appendix A: Tips and Tricks 239

Appendix B: Sample Questions 243

Index 245

About the Author

Piyush Sachdeva is an experienced DevOps and cloud specialist. He started his career in 2012 and had the privilege of working on cutting-edge cloud solutions in the industry. He currently works as a technical solutions developer at Google Canada, where he leverages his expertise in cloud services (GKE and Anthos as specializations) and automation. Throughout his career, he has earned 18+ cloud and DevOps certifications, including CKA certification in 2020 and 2024. Additionally, he has been honored to be an AWS Community Builder since 2021 and a HashiCorp Ambassador, contributing to the community by sharing knowledge and best practices.

He founded "The CloudOps Community," where students and working professionals learn and build cool stuff online. He also hosts monthly challenges that focus on learning and real-time hands-on tasks such as #40daysofkubernetes, #10weeksofcloudops, and more.

He also runs a YouTube channel, TechTutorialsWithPiyush, where he teaches everything from cloud platforms (AWS, Azure, GCP) to DevOps methodologies. His goal is to make complex topics accessible and help others grow in their tech journey.

About the Technical Reviewer

Shubham Londhe—a Developer Advocate at Amazon Web Services and DevOps specialist—brings his extensive industry knowledge to global audiences.

With over eight years of experience sharing real-world insights on topics like DevOps, cloud, and software engineering, Shubham has become a trusted mentor on YouTube and LinkedIn for his initiative of Train With Shubham.

He is passionate regarding making tech accessible for everyone, from beginners to advanced professionals, drawing on his background in both start-ups and midsize companies.

Acknowledgments

Writing *Certified Kubernetes Administrator Study Companion* has been a journey of deep learning, discipline, and focus. I would like to express my heartfelt gratitude to two mentors who, through their books, played a pivotal role in shaping my approach to productivity and consistency—Ali Abdaal and James Clear.

Ali Abdaal's *Feel-Good Productivity* taught me how to structure my work in a way that felt both enjoyable and sustainable, while James Clear's *Atomic Habits* helped me build systems that kept me on track, focusing on what truly matters. Their insights have been instrumental in helping me balance content creation, technical writing, and continuous learning.

Without the direction and mindset shifts I gained from their work, this book might have remained just an idea. Thank you for the wisdom and frameworks that made this possible.

Introduction

The CKA was created by the Linux Foundation and the Cloud Native Computing Foundation (CNCF) as a part of their ongoing effort to help develop the Kubernetes ecosystem. The exam is an online, proctored, performance-based test that requires solving multiple tasks from a command line running Kubernetes.

Once enrolled you will receive access to an exam simulator, provided by Killer.sh, allowing you to experience the exam environment. You will have two simulation attempts (36 hours of access for each attempt from the start of activation). The simulation includes 20–25 questions that are exactly the same for every attempt and every user, unlike the actual exam. The simulation will provide graded results.

—As per the Linux Foundation website

How This Book Is Organized

The Certified Kubernetes Administrator (CKA) exam tests your ability to deploy and manage production-grade Kubernetes clusters. In this book, I will deep-dive into each topic required for the exam and what a Kubernetes Administrator is expected to know. This book is divided into 6 parts and 23 chapters, each focusing on a particular area of Kubernetes, such as fundamentals and core concepts, workloads and scheduling, storage, installation, upgrades, maintenance, etc.

INTRODUCTION

The exam is not Multiple Choice Question (MCQ) based; rather, it is a complete hands-on one where you will be provided with a sandbox lab environment based on a Linux Ubuntu image, and you will be asked to perform certain tasks based on your learning. These could include simple tasks such as writing a kubectl command, intermediate tasks such as creating an Ingress based on the requirements, and advanced tasks such as Kubernetes cluster upgrade and installation. This book has been curated keeping in mind all the tasks that are important for the exam and from a Kubernetes Administrator point of view.

You will also notice that we will be doing two types of Kubernetes installation: one is KinD and the other is using Kubeadm. Both serve a specific purpose. We will be using KinD in the beginning to get you started without knowing much about Kubernetes' internal workings and troubleshooting aspects; however, in the latter part of the book, we will use a Kubeadm setup which will prepare you for more advanced topics. Instead of KinD, you can also use `Minikube`,[1] but KinD is recommended, as Minikube has some limitations and is heavy on your system as compared to KinD which is a lightweight Kubernetes distribution.

Prerequisites to Kubernetes

Kubernetes is one of the most popular container orchestration tools that enable businesses to build scalable and resilient applications. However, before diving into Kubernetes, it's essential to have a strong foundation in key technical areas.

---

[1] Minikube: A tool that allows users to set up a Kubernetes cluster on their local computer

INTRODUCTION

This book guides you through each of the Kubernetes topics from a beginner's perspective and from the CKA exam perspective; however, there are no prerequisites for the CKA exam.

Container Technology Proficiency: Master Docker/Podman, container networking, and troubleshooting.

Linux Administration Skills: Gain expertise in Linux, including systemd, process management, logging, network storage, etc.

Networking Concepts: Understand IP addressing, DNS, load balancing, and security protocols like SSL/TLS.

YAML and JSON Configuration: Learn the essential syntax for defining Kubernetes manifests.

Security Fundamentals: Familiarize yourself with authentication, PKI, RBAC, and service accounts.

Skill in Deploying Containers: Develop the ability to deploy and troubleshoot containerized applications.

INTRODUCTION

Figure 1 outlines the technical prerequisites you should acquire before learning Kubernetes, although there are no prerequisites for the CKA exam.

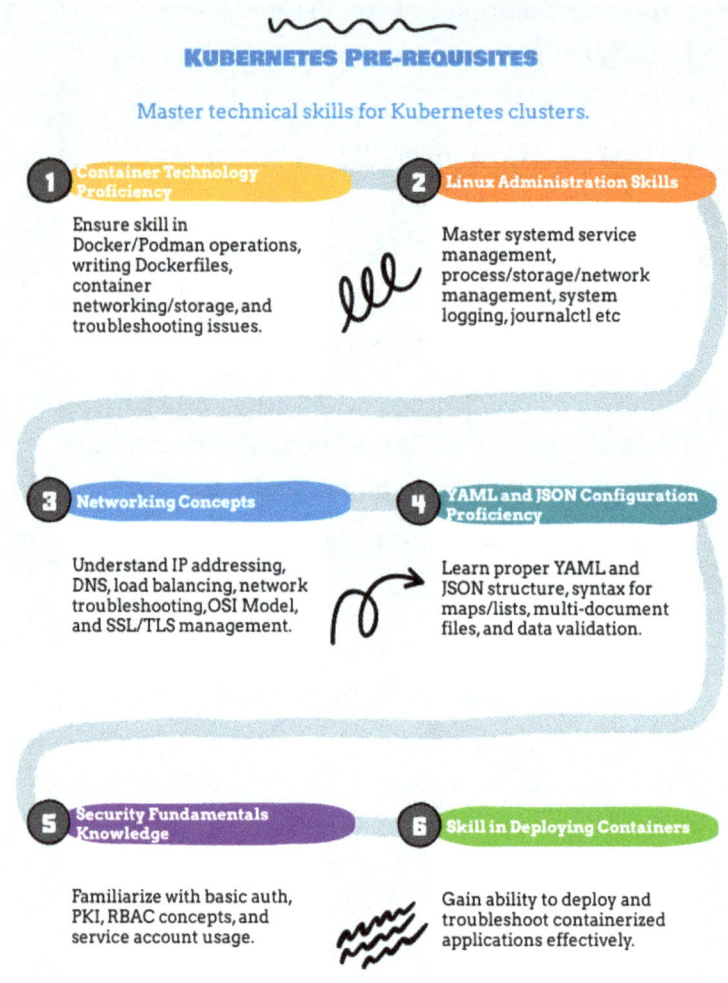

Figure 1. *Prerequisites to learning Kubernetes*

Exam Requirements

The CKA exam is online and proctored, so there are some requirements when it comes to supported OS, supported browser, system requirements, and so on. Make sure you go through the requirements outlined in the candidate handbook or the following link:

https://docs.linuxfoundation.org/tc-docs/certification/lf-handbook2/candidate-requirements

The minimum passing threshold is 66%. Questions carry different weights, based on their complexity and completion time.

When ready, register for the exam. All the details are available in the Linux Foundation exam handbook:

https://docs.linuxfoundation.org/tc-docs/certification/lf-handbook2

You will have two hours to complete between 15 and 20 practical tasks. Each task tests your ability to solve real Kubernetes administration challenges, so time management is crucial. Appendix A provides some tips on time management.

Figure 2 shows the distribution of tasks per topic for the CKA exam as per the latest Linux Foundation's syllabus.

INTRODUCTION

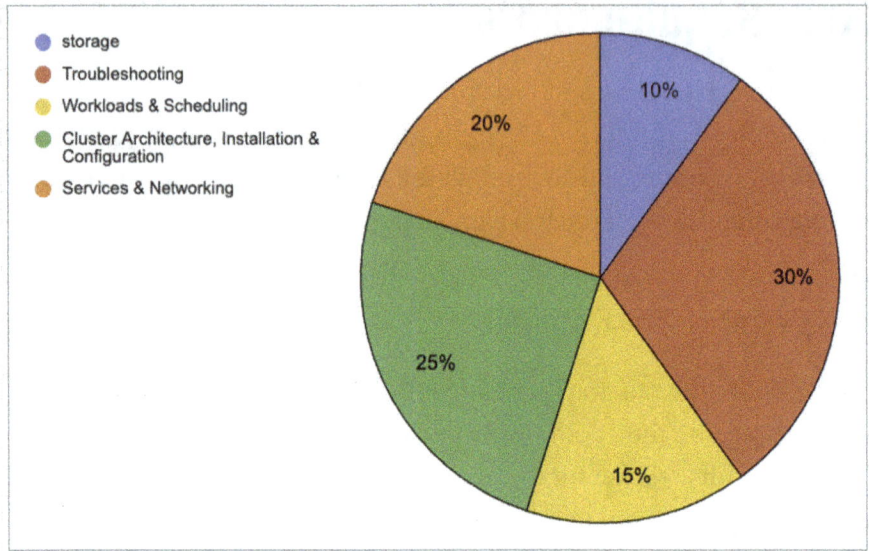

Figure 2. *Exam weightage per topic*

CKA Exam Changes

In February 2025, the Linux Foundation implemented some changes in the exam curriculum to better align it with the fast-evolving cloud and DevOps technologies. Although I have covered everything in this book as per the new curriculum, it is important to understand what has changed.

The following topics have been added.

Storage

- Implement StorageClasses and dynamic volume provisioning

Workloads and Scheduling

- Configure workload autoscaling (VPA, HPA)
- Configure pod admission and scheduling (limits, node affinity, etc.)

Services and Networking

- Define and enforce network policies
- Use the Gateway API to manage Ingress traffic

Cluster Maintenance, Installation, and Upgrades

- Implement and configure a highly available control plane
- Use Helm and Kustomize to install cluster components
- Understand extension interfaces (CNI, CSI, CRI, etc.)
- Understand CRDs and install and configure operators

The following topics have been removed:

- ETCD backup and restore
- Prepare underline infrastructure for the Kubernetes cluster

PART I

Kubernetes Fundamentals

Chapters 1–3 provide a solid introduction to Kubernetes, covering its purpose, core concepts, and architecture. This part begins with an overview of what Kubernetes is and why it's essential for managing containerized applications at scale. We will then look into the Kubernetes architecture, explaining the roles of control plane and worker nodes along with key components such as the API Server, etcd, Scheduler, Controller Managers, Kubelet, and container runtime. Finally, we will explore setting up both single-node and multi-node Kubernetes clusters using KinD, giving readers hands-on experience to reinforce their understanding.

CHAPTER 1

Introduction to Kubernetes

As microservices become more adaptable, we are rapidly moving toward containerization. However, merely running containers is insufficient for rapid development and seamless integration. In this chapter, we will explore the challenges of managing containerized applications at scale and introduce Kubernetes as a solution.

The Container Management Challenge

Consider a simple scenario: you have a small application comprising several containers running on a virtual machine. When everything works smoothly, your development and operations teams are satisfied. However, this setup faces several critical challenges.

CHAPTER 1   INTRODUCTION TO KUBERNETES

Container Failures

When a container fails—whether it's a frontend service, database, or backend component—it directly impacts users. While manual intervention by operations teams might work for small applications, this approach doesn't scale for several reasons:

- 24/7 coverage requirements across global time zones
- Increased operational costs for maintaining support teams
- Response time delays during off-hours
- Limited ability to handle multiple simultaneous failures

Scale and Complexity

As applications grow, these challenges multiply exponentially:

- Managing hundreds or thousands of containers becomes unsustainable manually.
- Multiple concurrent container failures require rapid and coordinated responses.
- Virtual machine failures (underline host) can bring down entire applications.
- Version/application upgrades across numerous containers become logistically complex.

Operational Challenges

Beyond basic container management, teams face additional operational hurdles:

1. **Service Discovery and Exposure**: Determining how to expose applications to users and manage routing
2. **Load Balancing**: Distributing traffic effectively across container instances
3. **Resource Management**: Allocating and optimizing compute resources
4. **High Availability**: Ensuring continuous service despite failures
5. **Security**: Managing access controls and network policies
6. **Networking**: Handling inter-container communication
7. **Monitoring and Logging**: Tracking system health and debugging issues

Enter Kubernetes

Kubernetes is an open source container orchestration platform that addresses these challenges by providing features such as

- Container scheduling and placement
- Service discovery and load balancing
- Self-healing through automatic restarts and replacements

- Horizontal scaling
- Rolling updates and rollbacks
- Resource management and optimization

When Not to Use Kubernetes

Despite its benefits, Kubernetes isn't always the right choice. Consider alternatives when

- Managing just a few containers
- Running simple applications with minimal scaling needs
- Operating with limited DevOps expertise
- Working with tight infrastructure budgets

For these cases, simpler solutions might be more appropriate:

- Docker Compose
- Single-host container deployments
- Virtual private servers
- Managed application platforms

CHAPTER 2

Kubernetes Architecture

Now that we have learned about the need for Kubernetes and the problems it solves, it's time to understand the Kubernetes architecture and its components.

Kubernetes architecture follows established distributed systems principles to provide a robust container orchestration platform. In this chapter, we will look into the core architectural components that enable Kubernetes to manage containerized applications at scale.

Figure 2-1 shows the Kubernetes architecture with one control plane and two worker nodes.

CHAPTER 2   KUBERNETES ARCHITECTURE

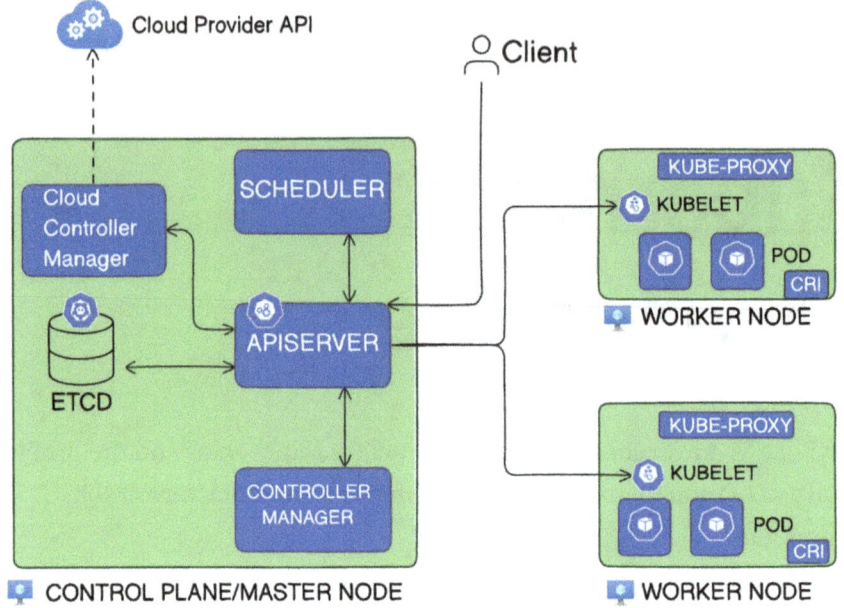

Figure 2-1. *Kubernetes architecture diagram*

Kubernetes implements a master-worker (control plane and data plane) architecture that separates cluster management functions from application workload execution.

Each of these components is deployed on separate **nodes** to ensure reliable cluster operations while maintaining scalability and fault tolerance.

Nodes

You might be wondering what exactly a node is in Kubernetes.

A Kubernetes node is nothing but a physical machine or a virtual machine with Kubernetes components installed on top of it and connected to form a Kubernetes cluster.

Control Plane vs. Worker Nodes

The architecture consists of two primary layers:

1. **Control Plane/Master Nodes**: Manages the cluster state and makes global decisions

2. **Data Plane/Worker Nodes**: Executes application workloads and implements networking policies

The *master node (a.k.a. control plane)* is the brain of the Kubernetes cluster. It manages the cluster's overall state, ensuring that the desired state (as defined by the user) matches the actual state of the cluster. The control plane components take care of all the operational and administrative tasks.

Worker nodes are the machine(s) where the actual application workloads (pods) run. They are responsible for running the containers and ensuring that the application remains highly available, fault tolerant, and highly scalable.

Control Plane Components

The control plane manages the cluster state and orchestrates all operations. Its key components include

- **API Server**: The primary management endpoint that accepts and processes all REST requests

- **ETCD**: A distributed key-value store that maintains cluster state

- **Kube-Scheduler**: Assigns workloads to worker nodes based on resource requirements

CHAPTER 2   KUBERNETES ARCHITECTURE

- **Controller Manager**: Manages various controllers that handle routine cluster operations

- **Cloud Control Manager**: Allows your API Server to interact with your cloud provider to manage and provision cloud resources

Each of these components serves a specific purpose in maintaining the desired cluster state; let's discuss the control plane components in more detail.

API Server

The Kubernetes API Server is a component of the Kubernetes control plane that exposes the Kubernetes API, which is used by all other components of Kubernetes and client applications (such as Kubectl, the CLI tool) to interact with the cluster. It acts as the frontend for the Kubernetes control plane, and the client interacts with the cluster using API Server. It is responsible for validating and processing API requests, maintaining the desired state of the cluster, and handling Kubernetes resources such as pods, services, replication controllers, and others.

API Server is the only control plane component that interacts with all other control plane components such as Scheduler, ETCD, Controller Manager, etc.

Figure 2-2 shows the architecture of Kubernetes control plane components.

CHAPTER 2 KUBERNETES ARCHITECTURE

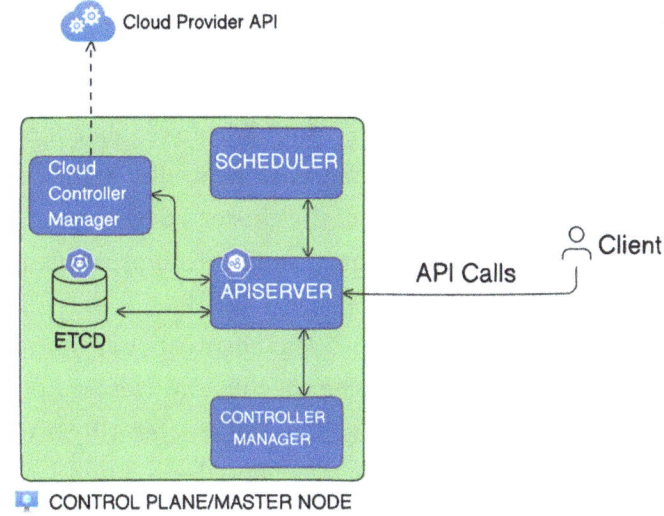

Figure 2-2. *Control plane components*

Kube-Scheduler

The Scheduler in Kubernetes is a component responsible for scheduling workloads (such as pods) to the nodes in the cluster. It watches for newly created pods with no assigned node, selects an appropriate node for each pod, assigns a rank to the node, and then binds the pod to that node.

The scheduler considers factors such as resource requirements, hardware/software constraints, affinity and anti-affinity specifications, labels and selectors, and other policies defined by the user or cluster administrator when making scheduling decisions.

These scheduling factors and variables will be discussed later in this book.

Controller Manager

The Controller Manager in Kubernetes is a component of the control plane that manages different types of controllers to regulate the state of the cluster and perform cluster-wide tasks. Each controller in the Controller Manager manages a specific aspect of the cluster's desired state, such as ReplicaSetController, DeploymentController, NamespaceController, NodeControllers, and others.

These controllers continuously work to ensure that the current state of the cluster matches the desired state specified by users or applications. They monitor the cluster state through the Kubernetes API Server, detect any differences between the current and desired states, and take corrective actions to reconcile them, such as creating or deleting resources as needed.

For instance, if a node becomes NotReady (Unhealthy), the NodeController takes the action of node repair and replaces it with a healthy node (if required).

ETCD Server

ETCD is a distributed key-value storage used as the primary datastore in Kubernetes for storing cluster state and configuration information. It is a critical component of the Kubernetes control plane that is responsible for storing information such as cluster configuration, the state of all Kubernetes objects (such as pods, services, and replication controllers), and information about nodes in the cluster. ETCD ensures consistency and reliability by using a distributed consensus algorithm to replicate data across multiple nodes in the ETCD cluster.

CHAPTER 2 KUBERNETES ARCHITECTURE

Cloud Controller Manager

The Cloud Controller Manager abstracts the cloud-specific details from the core Kubernetes components, allowing Kubernetes to be used across different cloud providers without requiring changes to the core Kubernetes codebase. In this book, we are not discussing the managed cloud services; hence, Cloud Controller Manager will not be discussed much.

Worker Node Components

Let's strengthen our understanding of the worker nodes by examining the essential components that enable them to run your applications. In this section, we will look into the critical roles of the Kubelet, Kube-proxy, and the Container Runtime, the backbone of pod execution and network communication on each node.

Kubelet

In Kubernetes, Kubelet is the primary node agent that runs on each node in the cluster. It is responsible for managing the containers running on the node and ensuring that they are healthy and running as expected.

Figure 2-3 shows the Kubelet pod lifecycle management.

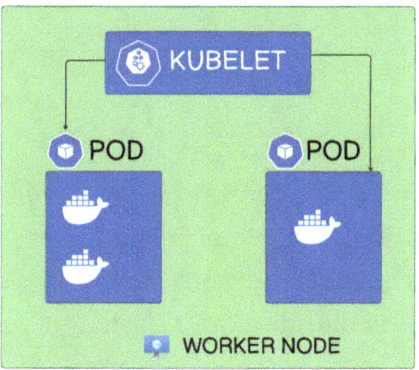

Figure 2-3. *Kubelet running on a worker node*

Some of the key responsibilities of Kubelet include

1. **Pod Lifecycle Management**: Kubelet is responsible for starting, stopping, and maintaining containers within a pod as directed by the Kubernetes API Server.

2. **Node Monitoring**: Kubelet monitors the health of the node and reports back to the Kubernetes control plane. If the node becomes unhealthy, the control plane can take corrective actions, such as rescheduling pods to other healthy nodes.

3. **Resource Management**: Kubelet manages the node's resources (CPU, memory, disk, etc.) and enforces resource limits and requests specified in pod configurations.

4. **Volume Management**: Kubelet manages pod volumes, including mounting and unmounting volumes as specified in the pod configuration.

Overall, Kubelet plays a crucial role in ensuring that pods are running correctly on each node in the Kubernetes cluster and that the cluster remains healthy and operational. While the Scheduler assigns pods to the node, the actual work of container execution is taken care of by the Kubelet.

kube-proxy

In Kubernetes, kube-proxy is a network proxy that runs on each node in the cluster. It is responsible for implementing part of the Kubernetes service concept, which enables network communication to your pods from network clients inside or outside of your cluster.

CHAPTER 2　KUBERNETES ARCHITECTURE

Figure 2-4 shows how kube-proxy helps with network communication with pods.

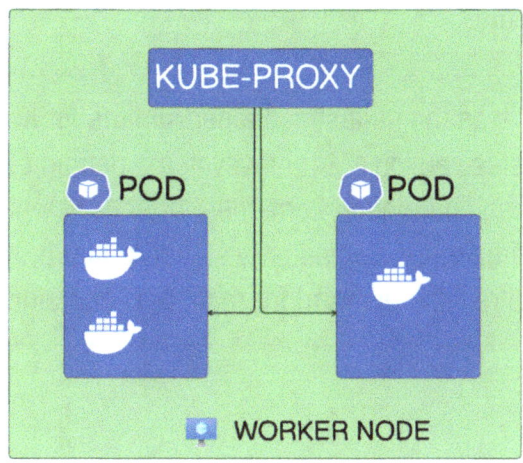

Figure 2-4. *kube-proxy running on a worker node*

kube-proxy maintains network rules on each node. These network rules allow network communication to be forwarded to the appropriate pod based on IP address and port number.

Container Runtime

In Kubernetes, a container runtime is the software responsible for running containers. It is an essential component of the Kubernetes architecture because Kubernetes itself does not run containers directly; instead, it relies on a container runtime to do so.

The container runtime is responsible for

1. Pulling container images from a container registry (e.g., Docker Hub, Artifact Registry)

2. Creating and managing container lifecycle (start, stop, pause, delete)

15

CHAPTER 2   KUBERNETES ARCHITECTURE

3. Managing container networking and storage

4. Providing container isolation and resource constraints

Note   Docker was the default container runtime for Kubernetes before Kubernetes version 1.24; however, the default container runtime has been changed to Containerd after 1.24 which is a **CRI** (container runtime interface) industry standard that provides a lightweight and reliable platform for managing containers.

Summary

- Kubernetes is a modern container orchestration platform that helps run your containerized workload at scale.

- Kubernetes implements a master-worker-based architecture in which master or control plane nodes are responsible for administrative and operational tasks and worker nodes are responsible for running customer workloads.

Control plane components include

- **API Server**: The primary process that processes all incoming requests and communicates with other components

- **ETCD**: A distributed key-value store that maintains cluster state

- **Kube-Scheduler**: Assigns workloads to worker nodes based on resource requirements
- **Controller Manager**: Manages various controllers that handle routine cluster operations

Worker node components include

- **Kubelet**: The node agent that runs on each node and makes sure that containers are running in a pod.
- **kube-proxy**: Maintains network rules that enable communication to your pods from inside or outside the cluster.
- **Container Runtime**: Maintains the execution and lifecycle of a container. Containerd is the default container runtime after Kubernetes version 1.24; earlier, it was Docker.

CHAPTER 3

Kubernetes Installation

In the previous chapter, we have learned about the Kubernetes architecture and its components; now it's time to see those concepts in action by performing the Kubernetes installation.

A Kubernetes cluster including its control plane components can be deployed in several ways, and the installation type depends on your use case, budget, and requirements.

Figure 3-1 shows the available options for a Kubernetes cluster set up based on the requirements.

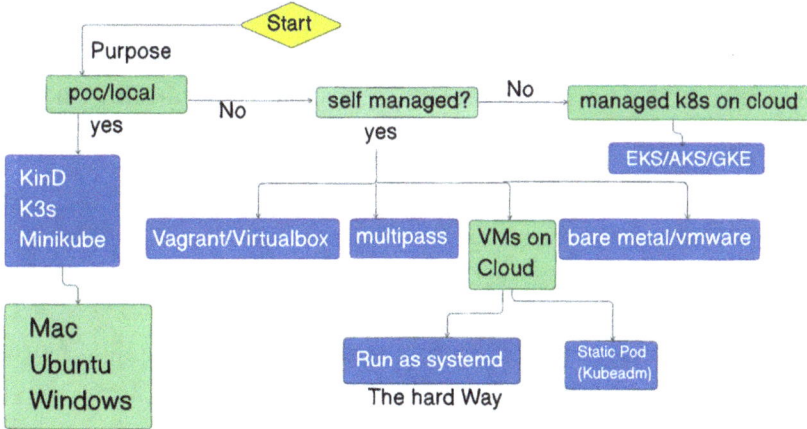

Figure 3-1. *Kubernetes cluster installation options*

If you are doing a Proof of Concept (POC) or using the cluster for learning purposes or testing something, then you can use either Minikube, KinD, or K3S. You cannot do a lot of things in Minikube as it does not support network policies; hence, we will be starting with KinD, which is Kubernetes inside Docker.

In your local machine, with Docker installed, it will provision multiple containers for you, and each of these containers will act as a separate node of the cluster, hence the name KinD. In the first half of this book, we will be working with the KinD cluster; however, once you are familiar with Kubernetes, we will be running the cluster components as static pods using Kubeadm so that we can work on advanced Kubernetes concepts such as Kubernetes installation, upgrade, network policies, and so on.

In this chapter, we'll be performing both Kubernetes single-node and multi-node installation using KinD.

Kubernetes Single-Node Installation Using KinD

Prerequisites

Make sure you have Go 1.16+ and Docker installed and running on your machine to run and use KinD.

Installation

To create a cluster using KinD, you need to first install KinD. There are several options, such as installing from release binaries, installation from source, or using a package manager. You can follow the below document for up-to-date instructions:

```
https://kind.sigs.k8s.io/docs/user/quick-start
```

CHAPTER 3 KUBERNETES INSTALLATION

To create a cluster using the latest kind image, you can use the below command:

```
kind create cluster --name cka-cluster
```

Optionally, you can pass the –image parameter to the command to install a specific version, for example:

```
kind create cluster --image \ kindest/node:v1.29.4@sha256:3abb816a5b1061fb15c6e9e60856ec40d56b7b52bcea5f5f1350bc6e2320b6f8 --name \ cka-cluster1
```

Figure 3-2 shows the terminal output after running the kind create cluster command.

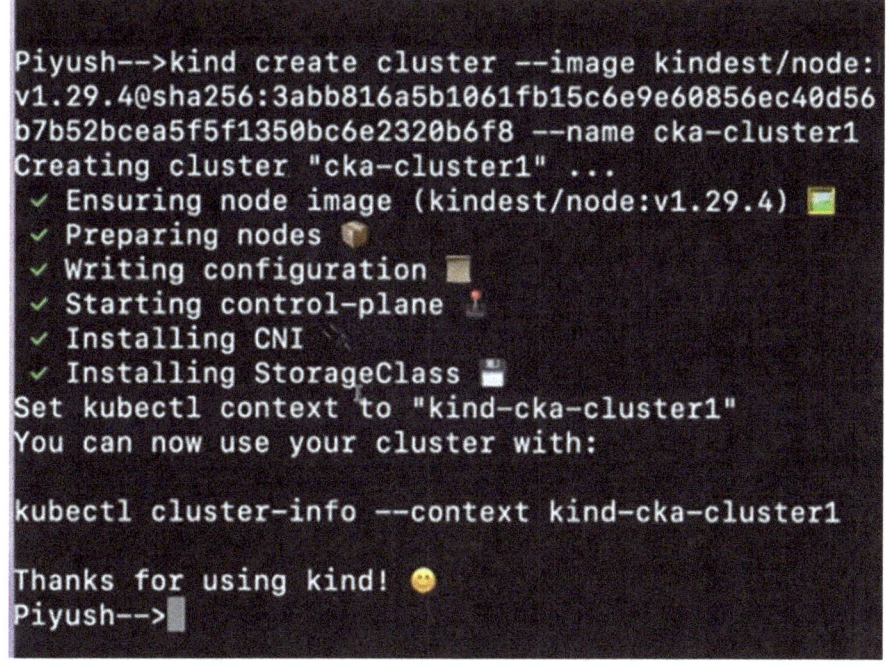

Figure 3-2. *KinD cluster create output*

CHAPTER 3   KUBERNETES INSTALLATION

Kubernetes Multi-node Installation Using KinD

To create a multi-node cluster with multiple control plane and multiple worker nodes, you can use a config.yaml file as below:

```
# Three node (two workers) cluster config
kind: Cluster
apiVersion: kind.x-k8s.io/v1alpha4 # apiVersion could change in the future release; hence, validate from the official kind documentation
nodes:
- role: control-plane
- role: worker
- role: worker
```

You can add more control plane and worker nodes by adding more elements in the nodes section of the config YAML and finally running the below command to create the cluster:

```
kind create cluster --config config.yaml --name cka-cluster-2
```

To see all the clusters you have created, you can use the command

```
kind get clusters
```

which should give you results of clusters you have created with KinD, for example:

```
cka-cluster1
cka-cluster2
```

To interact with the cluster, you should already have Kubectl utility installed on your machine; if you do not have it, now is the good time to install it by going to the following link:

https://kubernetes.io/docs/tasks/tools/install-kubectl-linux/

CHAPTER 3 KUBERNETES INSTALLATION

kubectl is a command-line tool that helps communicate with the Kubernetes control plane using the Kubernetes API. It uses a file called kubeconfig located in the $HOME/.kube directory by default, and you can override the file by setting the KUBECONFIG environment variable or by setting the –kubeconfig flag in the kubectl commands.

To interact with a specific cluster, you only need to specify the cluster name as a context in Kubectl:

```
kubectl cluster-info --context kind-kind
kubectl cluster-info --context kind-kind-2
```

Now, you can run the kubectl command against your cluster; to get the nodes, you can execute the below command which should show the node details, including its status, role, name, age, and the Kubernetes version. If you have done the setup properly, the nodes should be in Ready status.

```
kubectl get nodes
```

Figure 3-3 shows the sample output after running the kubectl get nodes command on the terminal.

```
Piyush-->kubectl get nodes
NAME                          STATUS   ROLES           AGE   VERSION
cka-cluster2-control-plane    Ready    control-plane   91s   v1.29.4
cka-cluster2-worker           Ready    <none>          66s   v1.29.4
cka-cluster2-worker2          Ready    <none>          67s   v1.29.4
Piyush-->
```

Figure 3-3. *Verify cluster health*

To delete the cluster, replace the create keyword in the command with delete as below:

```
kind delete cluster -name cka-cluster1
```

Remember, these are nothing but the containers running on your machine.

Summary

- A Kubernetes cluster can be deployed in several ways such as KinD, Minikube, K3S, self-managed, VMs on Cloud, systemd processes, static pods, or even the managed services by cloud providers, such as AKS, EKS, GKE, etc.

- We can quickly set up a Kubernetes cluster locally using KinD which creates multiple containers, and each container acts as a Kubernetes node that forms a cluster.

- Once the cluster is created, you can interact by switching the context to the cluster name. The kubectl utility is a prerequisite to be installed on the machine to interact with the cluster.

- You can run the `kubectl get nodes` command to verify that your cluster installation is successful.

PART II

Workloads and Scheduling

These topics cover 15% of the exam and focus on the following:

- Understanding deployments and how to perform rolling update and rollbacks
- Using configmaps and Secrets to configure applications
- Configuring workload autoscaling
- Configuring pod admission and scheduling (limits, node affinity, etc.)
- Knowing how to scale applications
- Understanding the primitives used to create robust, self-healing, application deployments
- Understanding how resource limits can affect pod scheduling
- Awareness of manifest management and common templating tools

CHAPTER 4

Pods in Kubernetes

So far, we have done the cluster installation and understood the Kubernetes fundamentals. From this chapter onward, we will be doing the hands-on with actual Kubernetes resources starting with pods.

Pods are the smallest deployable units that you can create and manage in Kubernetes. You run your applications on these Kubernetes pods.

Figure 4-1 shows the representation of a pod inside the Kubernetes cluster.

Figure 4-1. *Pod running in the cluster*

CHAPTER 4   PODS IN KUBERNETES

A pod is a group of one or more containers, with shared storage and network resources, and a specification for how to run the containers. Ideally, you should have one container per pod; however, there are some edge cases (we will discuss those later in this chapter) in which you need to use multiple containers inside a pod.

There are a couple of ways to create Kubernetes objects such as pod:

- **Imperative Way**: Through Kubectl commands or API calls

- **Declarative Way**: By creating manifest files (usually in YAML or JSON format) with the desired state

Imperative Way

You can create a pod or any supported Kubernetes object using a simple kubectl command such as

```
kubectl run <podname> --image=<imagename:tag>
```

To check the status of running pods, you can simply run

```
kubectl get pods
```

Figure 4-2 shows the output of pod creation using the kubectl command (imperative way).

```
Piyush--->kubectl run nginx-pod --image=nginx:latest
pod/nginx-pod created
Piyush--->kubectl get pods
NAME          READY   STATUS    RESTARTS   AGE
nginx-pod     1/1     Running   0          10s
Piyush--->
```

Figure 4-2. Create a pod using kubectl

CHAPTER 4 PODS IN KUBERNETES

Declarative Way

Creating a Kubernetes object such as a pod through the manifest file can be done using a YAML or JSON file. (YAML is the preferred way.)

Below is a sample YAML that can be used to create an nginx pod that exposes an nginx container on port 80:

```
apiVersion: v1
kind: Pod
metadata:
  name: nginx-pod
  labels:
    env: demo
    type: frontend
spec:
  containers:
  - name: nginx-container
    image: nginx
    ports:
    - containerPort: 80
```

Most of the manifest YAMLs would have four mandatory top-level fields such as apiVersion, kind, metadata, and spec (as highlighted above).

Once the file is created with .yaml or .yml extension, you can simply run the `kubectl create -f filename` command to apply the changes. To make changes in the pod specification such as label, container, etc., you need to update the file and apply it again using `kubectl apply -f filename`.

The apply parameter in the command can be used to create a new object or to make changes to the existing object; however, create can only be used to create new objects. Most of the Kubernetes admins use only the apply command instead of create.

Figure 4-3 shows the terminal output of a pod creation using the declarative way (by applying a manifest yaml).

```
Piyush--->kubectl create -f pod.yaml
pod/nginx-pod created
Piyush--->kubectl get pods
NAME         READY   STATUS    RESTARTS   AGE
nginx-pod    1/1     Running   0          4s
```

Figure 4-3. *Create a pod using the declarative way*

Pod Lifecycle

Each pod in Kubernetes progresses through distinct phases that summarize its state:

> **Pending**: The pod is accepted by the cluster but is waiting for scheduling and not yet running.
>
> **Running**: The pod is assigned to a node, and at least one container is running or starting.
>
> **Succeeded**: All containers have completed successfully.
>
> **Failed**: One or more containers have failed, and the pod will not restart.
>
> **Unknown**: The pod state cannot be determined due to a node communication failure.

Figure 4-4 shows the lifecycle of a pod in Kubernetes.

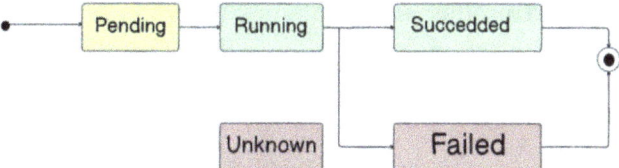

Figure 4-4. Pod lifecycle

Container States in a Pod

Inside a pod, each container has its own lifecycle, categorized into three states:

> **Waiting**: The container is preparing to start, pulling images, or processing secrets.
>
> **Running**: The container is actively executing without errors.
>
> **Terminated**: The container has either successfully exited or failed, with logs indicating the reason.

Inspect the Pods

To inspect the pods if it is throwing an error, you can use the below commands to check the events and associated error logs, respectively:

```
kubectl describe pod podname
kubectl logs podname
```

To make changes to a running pod, you can edit the manifest file and apply the changes through the `kubectl apply` command, or you can also directly run the `kubectl edit pod <podname>` command to edit the live object without making any changes to the manifest file.

To log in to the running pod's container, you can use the `kubectl exec` command which is similar to performing an SSH into the container:

```
kubectl exec -it nginx-pod --sh
```

To create a YAML with the pre-populated fields that can be used to create a new pod, you can use the below commands to first `dry-run` the kubectl command and then redirect the output to a sample yaml file:

Figure 4-5 shows the terminal output after running the kubectl command for dry-run.

```
Piyush—>kubectl run nginx --image=nginx --dry-run=client
pod/nginx created (dry run)
Piyush—>kubectl run nginx --image=nginx --dry-run=client -o yaml
```

Figure 4-5. *Dry-run command to get the YAML*

Similarly, you can redirect the output into a JSON file instead of YAML by changing the last flag to json as below:

```
kubectl run nginx --image=nginx -dry-run=client -o json
```

If you want to check the details about a running pod, you can perform a kubectl describe on the pod and look for a particular field, and the below commands will also show some additional details, such as the node name where the pod is running and labels, respectively.

```
kubectl get pods -o wide
kubectl get pods nginx-pod --show-labels
```

Multi-container Pods

Pods can have multiple containers that need to work together in cases where containers are tightly coupled and need to share resources. Multi-container pods include init containers and sidecar/helper containers:

CHAPTER 4   PODS IN KUBERNETES

Init Containers: Run and complete before the application containers are started, for instance, to perform some pre-validation/sanity checks or operations

Sidecar Containers: Provide some helper service to the main application container, for example, service mesh, monitoring agent, logging agent, etc.

Figure 4-6 shows the representation of a multi-container pod inside a Kubernetes cluster.

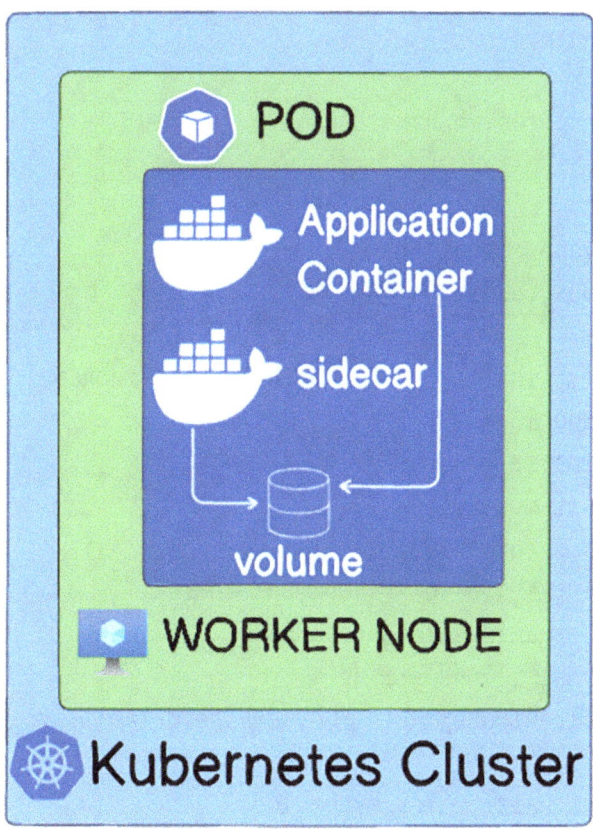

Figure 4-6. *Nginx container running with a sidecar container*

33

CHAPTER 4   PODS IN KUBERNETES

We have already learned a brief introduction about multi-container pods; let us see how we can create such pods. For instance, we have to create a multi-container pod with nginx as the main application container and an init container that checks for service availability and completes when the service is up and running. We will be learning about services in Chapter 6, but, for now, let's just focus on the multi-container pod.

Here's a sample YAML for a multi-container pod:

```yaml
apiVersion: v1
kind: Pod
metadata:
  name: myapp-pod
  labels:
    app.kubernetes.io/name: MyApp
spec:
  containers:
  - name: myapp-container
    image: busybox:1.28
    env:
    command: ['sh', '-c', 'echo The app is running! &&
    sleep 3600']
  initContainers:
  - name: init-myservice
    image: busybox:1.28
    command: ['sh', '-c'] # command to run
    args: # arguments to the command
      - > # multi-line string
        until nslookup          myservice.default.svc.cluster.
                                local; do
         echo waiting for myservice;
          sleep 2;
        done;
```

34

When you apply the yaml, the init container will be executed first and look for the service after every two seconds; as soon as the service is created and accessible, it will be completed, and the app container will be started. During this time, the pod status will be init[0/1] as the init container is still waiting to be finished.

Prior to Kubernetes 1.28, sidecars were essentially just regular containers that ran alongside the main application. With Kubernetes 1.28 (and default in 1.29+), a more formal sidecar concept emerged, which involves defining them within initContainers but with a restartPolicy: Always. This allows them to start before the main app but continue running and also allows them to use probes.

Environment Variables in Kubernetes

To reuse the same variables inside the container multiple times, we can use environment variables. We define the variable inside the container with the field named env and key-value pair with name and value. The variable can then be accessed with a $ sign inside the container.

```
apiVersion: v1
kind: Pod
metadata:
  name: myapp-pod
spec:
  containers:
  - name: myapp-container
    image: busybox:1.28
    env:
    - name: FIRSTNAME
      value: "Piyush"
    command: ['sh', '-c', 'echo Hello my name is $FIRSTNAME! && sleep 3600']
```

CHAPTER 4   PODS IN KUBERNETES

Summary

- Pods are the smallest deployable units in Kubernetes, designed to run one or more containers with shared storage, network, and runtime specifications. While a single container per pod is common, multi-container pods can also be used for some use cases.

- You can create a pod using an imperative approach or a declarative approach.

- **Imperative Approach**: Use kubectl commands to create pods.

- **Declarative Approach**: Use YAML/JSON manifest files to define and manage pods. Apply changes with the command kubectl apply.

- Multi-container pods can be used for scenarios like logging, monitoring, or pre-start checks.

- **Init Containers**: Perform setup tasks before the main container starts.

- **Sidecar Containers**: Provide auxiliary services like logging agents.

- Environment variables are defined in the env section of pod specs as key-value pairs and accessed inside containers using $<variable_name>.

CHAPTER 5

ReplicaSets, Replication Controller, and Deployments

In this chapter, we will look into the core Kubernetes controllers responsible for maintaining application availability and scalability: Replication Controllers, ReplicaSets, and deployments. We will learn how these resources ensure that the desired number of pod replicas is always running and how deployments provide a higher-level abstraction for managing updates and rollbacks.

Replication Controller

We have learned about pods (the smallest deployable unit) in Kubernetes, which do not guarantee high availability and fault tolerance, as there is only a single copy of the container running all the time, and it is not backed by a controller that ensures that the pod is auto-healed upon failure.

To overcome the issue, the Replication Controller was created, which ensures that a specified number of pod replicas are up and running all the time. If there is a pod failure, the controller replaces the failed pod with a healthy pod to maintain the desired number of running replicas.

CHAPTER 5   REPLICASETS, REPLICATION CONTROLLER, AND DEPLOYMENTS

Replication Controllers are legacy controllers and are replaced by ReplicaSets managed by deployments, so we will focus more on ReplicaSets and deployments.

ReplicaSet

A ReplicaSet ensures that a given number of pod replicas are running all the time, ensuring high availability of the application. A ReplicaSet is the newer version of the Replication Controller and is mostly used along with the deployment, as it provides some additional features such as rolling updates. Usually, you define a deployment that manages a ReplicaSet automatically, and you do not interact with the ReplicaSet manually.

Figure 5-1 shows the architectural diagram and hierarchy of a ReplicaSet inside a Kubernetes container.

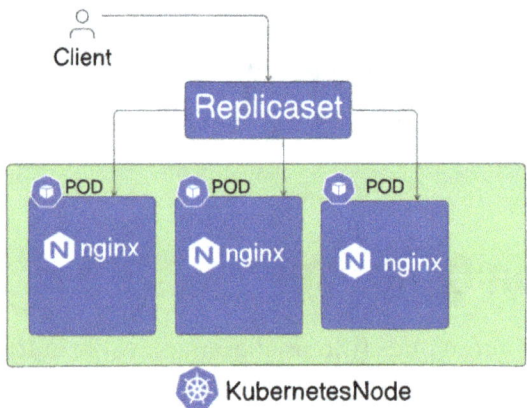

Figure 5-1. *Kubernetes ReplicaSet*

CHAPTER 5   REPLICASETS, REPLICATION CONTROLLER, AND DEPLOYMENTS

Deployment

A deployment provides declarative updates for pods and ReplicaSets. You describe a desired state in a deployment, and the deployment controller changes the actual state to match the desired state at a controlled rate.

You specify the pods inside the deployment using a template, and the ReplicaSet will be created automatically by the ReplicaSet Controller (a component of Kube-Controller Manager), which manages those pods. You also define the number of replicas inside the YAML that ensures a certain number of pods running all the time.

Figure 5-2 shows the architectural diagram of a deployment and hierarchy inside the Kubernetes cluster.

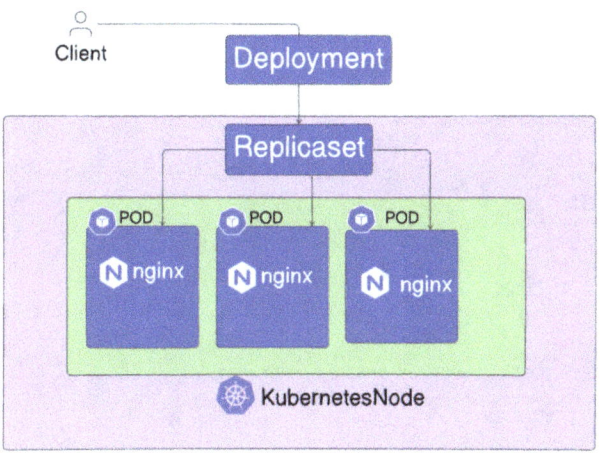

Figure 5-2. *Kubernetes deployment diagram*

While working with pods, we used `v1` as the `apiVersion`, but that is not the same for each of the Kubernetes objects. For deployment, we use the version as apps/v1; this field can be verified using the command `kubectl explain deployment`.

With the deployment, you are creating multiple replicas of a pod template; hence, you need to define the template inside the deployment manifest YAML. This template (highlighted in bold) is similar to the metadata and spec field of a pod YAML:

```
apiVersion: apps/v1
kind: Deployment
metadata:
  name: nginx-deployment
  labels:
    app: nginx
spec:
  replicas: 3
  selector:
    matchLabels:
      app: nginx
  template:
    metadata:
      labels:
        app: nginx
    spec:
      containers:
      - name: nginx
        image: nginx:latest
        ports:
        - containerPort: 80
```

The deployment YAML also contains two additional fields such as replicas and selector:

> **Replicas** defines the number of pod replicas, that is, the desired number of application instances that should be running all the time.

CHAPTER 5 REPLICASETS, REPLICATION CONTROLLER, AND DEPLOYMENTS

Selector defines the pod that the deployment manages based on the labels. The `matchLabels` suggests to control the pod that has a matching label, `env: demo` in this case.

Once you have created the yaml, it can be applied using the command

`kubectl apply -f <filename>`

Let's assume we have created the deployment with three replicas as stated above. It will create three pods and one deployment along with a ReplicaSet. You can check the status using the command `kubectl get pods` (po for short) or `kubectl get deployment` (deploy for short).

To check all the Kubernetes resources running in the cluster, you can run the command

`kubectl get all`

Figure 5-3 shows the terminal output of the kubectl get all command to check all the running resources in the cluster.

```
Piyush—>kubectl get all
NAME                                         READY   STATUS    RESTARTS   AGE
pod/nginx-deploy-5699c786d4-4m6tc            1/1     Running   0          36s
pod/nginx-deploy-5699c786d4-q9bc7            1/1     Running   0          36s
pod/nginx-deploy-5699c786d4-vjlqt            1/1     Running   0          36s

NAME                  TYPE        CLUSTER-IP   EXTERNAL-IP   PORT(S)
service/kubernetes    ClusterIP   10.96.0.1    <none>        443/TCP

NAME                              READY   UP-TO-DATE   AVAILABLE   AGE
deployment.apps/nginx-deploy      3/3     3            3           36s

NAME                                            DESIRED   CURRENT   READY
replicaset.apps/nginx-deploy-5699c786d4         3         3         3
Piyush—>
```

Figure 5-3. *Validate all the running resources in the cluster*

CHAPTER 5   REPLICASETS, REPLICATION CONTROLLER, AND DEPLOYMENTS

If you delete any of the running pods, the deployment controller will start another pod to match the desired state with the current state. If you want to perform cleanup, you need to delete the deployment itself using the command

```
kubectl delete deploy <deployment name>
```

How to Perform Rolling Updates/Rollback

If you would like to update the container image from one version to another, you can either use the command

```
kubectl edit deploy/deploymentname
```

and save the file opened in the vi editor or edit the YAML file, or there's another way using the kubectl command as below (\ at the end is the newline character):

```
kubectl set image deploy/nginx-deploy \ nginx=nginx:1.9.1
```

Figure 5-4 shows the terminal output of updating a container image through the kubectl command.

```
Piyush--->kubectl set image deploy/nginx-deploy \
> nginx=nginx:1.9.1
deployment.apps/nginx-deploy image updated
Piyush--->
```

Figure 5-4. *Update container image through kubectl*

Similarly, you can scale the number of replicas using the `kubectl scale` command as below:

```
kubectl scale --replicas=3 deployment/nginx-deploy
```

CHAPTER 5   REPLICASETS, REPLICATION CONTROLLER, AND DEPLOYMENTS

If you make any changes to the deployment, it creates a new deployment revision and can be checked using the rollout command:

```
kubectl rollout history deploy/nginx-deploy
```

Figure 5-5 shows the terminal output of the rollout history.

```
Piyush--->kubectl rollout history deploy/nginx-deploy
deployment.apps/nginx-deploy
REVISION   CHANGE-CAUSE
1          <none>
2          <none>
```

Figure 5-5. *Deployment revision history*

To revert the latest changes, you can use the `rollout undo` command or `rollout undo -revision` to undo a particular rollout revision number, for example:

```
kubectl rollout undo deploy/nginx-deploy
```

Figure 5-6 shows how to undo the latest rollout through kubectl.

```
Piyush--->kubectl rollout undo deploy/nginx-deploy
deployment.apps/nginx-deploy rolled back
```

Figure 5-6. *Undo the latest changes to a deployment*

Whenever you make any changes, the replicas are updated in a rolling update fashion by default, meaning it updates one replica at a time and keeps the other replicas running while changes are being performed on one replica. Kubernetes also supports another deployment strategy called **recreate**; as the name suggests, it replaces all the pods at once with newer pods, which could introduce some disruption to the application's availability.

CHAPTER 5   REPLICASETS, REPLICATION CONTROLLER, AND DEPLOYMENTS

To create a deployment using the imperative command, you can use the following:

```
kubectl create deploy nginx --image=nginx:latest
```

These commands are hard to remember especially for a beginner; the below quick-reference guide will come in handy for frequently used kubectl commands.

Note   The best part is that the guide along with the Kubernetes official documentation is accessible during the exam.

https://kubernetes.io/docs/reference/kubectl/quick-reference/

https://kubernetes.io/docs is available during the exam, including its subdomains such as https://kubernetes.io/docs/reference/kubectl/quick-reference/.

Summary

- **Replication Controller (Legacy)**: A legacy controller that maintains pod replicas and provides auto-healing capabilities; replaced by ReplicaSet but still supported in Kubernetes.

- **ReplicaSet**: A modern replacement for the Replication Controller that maintains desired pod replicas, provides high availability, and integrates with deployments.

CHAPTER 5   REPLICASETS, REPLICATION CONTROLLER, AND DEPLOYMENTS

- **Deployment**: A declarative controller that manages ReplicaSets automatically, handles pod updates/rollbacks, and ensures that the desired number of pod replicas is always up and running.

- **Useful Commands**

    ```
    # to create a deployment
    kubectl create deploy nginx --image=nginx:latest
    # to check the Kubernetes objects.
    kubectl get deploy
    kubectl get rs
    kubectl get pods
    kubectl get all
    # to perform rolling updates
    kubectl set image deploy/nginx-deploy nginx=nginx:1.9.1
    # to check the rollout history
    kubectl rollout history deploy/nginx-deploy
    # to undo the rollout changes
    kubectl rollout undo deploy/nginx-deploy
    kubectl rollout undo deploy/nginx-deploy --to-revision <revision_number>
    ```

- Deployments are the recommended way to manage ReplicaSets and pods, using RollingUpdate by default, with matching labels/selectors required.

CHAPTER 6

Services in Kubernetes

We create pods where we run our workloads for a frontend application. We create a deployment to make sure the pods are highly available. To ensure application pods are accessible to the outside world or to client applications, we need to expose the application as a service on an endpoint even when the workload is split across multiple backends. The service then acts as a load balancer, receives the incoming requests, and redirects them to the backend pods. In this chapter, we'll review the following four types of Kubernetes services:

- ClusterIP (for internal access)
- NodePort (to access the application on a particular port)
- Load Balancer (to access the application on a domain name or IP address without using the port number)
- External (to use an external DNS for routing)

CHAPTER 6   SERVICES IN KUBERNETES

ClusterIP

ClusterIP is the default service type in Kubernetes that makes your application accessible only within the Kubernetes cluster using an internal IP address. Other services within the cluster can use this IP to communicate with the service, for example, if you have a multi-tier application deployed as a pod with a frontend deployment, backend, and database. You can use ClusterIP to keep communication between multiple tiers without exposing the service externally.

Figure 6-1 shows a sample architecture of a three-tier application with ClusterIP service used for the backend pods.

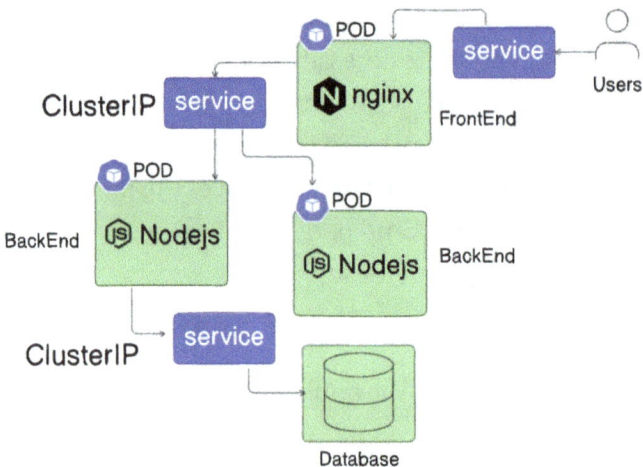

Figure 6-1. *Sample three-tier application that uses ClusterIP*

To expose a pod or deployment, you can use the below imperative command:

```
kubectl expose pod nginx --port=80
```

48

CHAPTER 6 SERVICES IN KUBERNETES

You can also use the below service YAML (declarative approach). It matches the service selector label with the deployment label and exposes it on an internal IP address. As ClusterIP is the default service type, we don't need to specify the service type, but we can add type:clusterIP inside the spec field.

```
apiVersion: v1
kind: Service
metadata:
  name: cluster-svc
  labels:
    env: demo
spec:
  ports:
  - port: 80
  selector:
    env: demo
```

NodePort

NodePort exposes the service on a specific port on each node in the cluster that allows external traffic to access the service by sending requests to <NodeIP>:<NodePort> where the NodePort is typically between 30000 and 32767.

In the NodePort, we usually deal with three types of ports:

- **NodePort**: The port of the service that is exposed externally
- **Internal Service Port**: The port on which the service is exposed internally
- **TargetPort**: The port on which your application is running

49

Figure 6-2 shows the representation of NodePort service in a Kubernetes cluster.

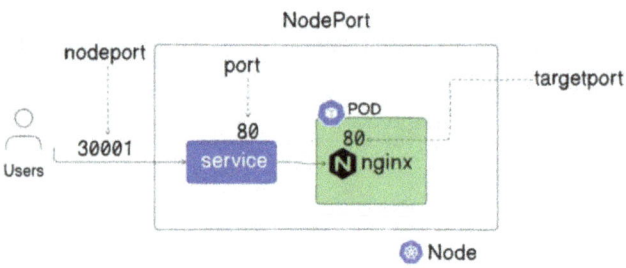

Figure 6-2. NodePort service in Kubernetes

Note If you are using a KinD cluster, we need to perform an extra step. If you remember, the nodes in the KinD are the containers running on your local machine, so we need to expose the nodes (containers) to use the service. You can delete the existing KinD cluster and create a new one using the below sample config yaml with extraPortMappings (for port forwarding), as you cannot update the existing KinD cluster.

```
kind: Cluster
apiVersion: kind.x-k8s.io/v1alpha4
nodes:
- role: control-plane
  extraPortMappings:
  - containerPort: 30001
    hostPort: 30001
- role: worker
- role: worker
```

CHAPTER 6　SERVICES IN KUBERNETES

Once you create the cluster with extraPortMapping, you can create the service YAML with the type as NodePort and specify the ports as below:

```
apiVersion: v1
kind: Service
metadata:
  name: nodeport-svc
  labels:
    env: demo
spec:
  type: NodePort
  ports:
  - nodePort: 30001
    port: 80
    targetPort: 80
  selector:
    env: demo
```

You can check the service status by running the kubectl command as below:

```
kubectl get svc or kubectl get service
```

Figure 6-3 shows the terminal output of all running services.

```
Piyush--->kubectl get svc
NAME            TYPE         CLUSTER-IP     EXTERNAL-IP    PORT(S)
kubernetes      ClusterIP    10.96.0.1      <none>         443/TCP
nodeport-svc    NodePort     10.96.59.97    <none>         80:30001/TCP
```

Figure 6-3. *Running services in the Kubernetes cluster*

Additionally, the command `kubectl describe svc nodeport-svc` shows the additional details such as IP addresses, endpoints, port details, labels, selectors, etc.

Figure 6-4 shows the terminal output of a service inspection in Kubernetes.

```
Piyush--->kubectl describe svc nodeport-svc
Name:                     nodeport-svc
Namespace:                default
Labels:                   env=demo
Annotations:              <none>
Selector:                 env=demo
Type:                     NodePort
IP Family Policy:         SingleStack
IP Families:              IPv4
IP:                       10.96.59.97
IPs:                      10.96.59.97
Port:                     <unset>  80/TCP
TargetPort:               80/TCP
NodePort:                 <unset>  30001/TCP
Endpoints:                10.244.1.2:80,10.244.1.3:80,10.244.2.2:80
```

Figure 6-4. *Inspect a Kubernetes service*

To test if your service is working fine, you can run a `curl localhost:30001`, which should redirect to the pod (running nginx) that was exposed with the service on port 30001 and return the default nginx home page.

Load Balancer

As the name suggests, this service will provision an external-facing load balancer with the help of `Cloud Controller Manager (CCM)` for your application and expose it via a public IP. Your load balancer service will act as `NodePort` if you are not using any managed cloud Kubernetes, such as *GKE*, *AKS*, *EKS*, etc. In a managed cloud environment, Kubernetes creates a load balancer within the cloud project, which redirects the traffic to the Kubernetes Load Balancer service.

Figure 6-5 shows how a Load Balancer service is used in a sample web application.

CHAPTER 6 SERVICES IN KUBERNETES

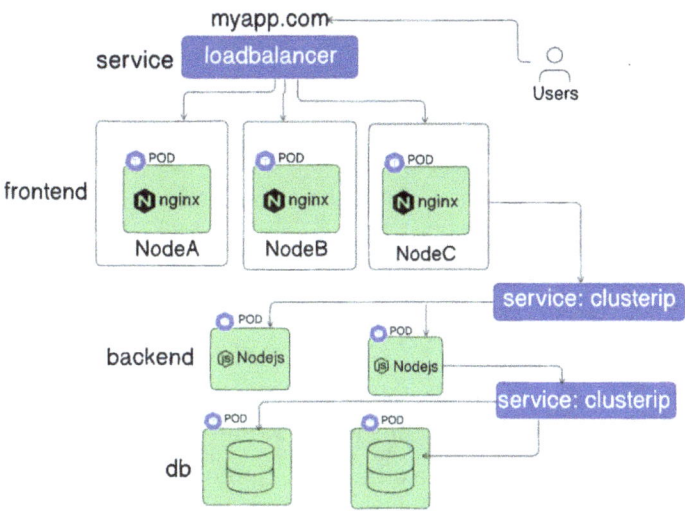

Figure 6-5. *Load Balancer service type in Kubernetes*

If you're deploying a production application that needs to be accessible to the outside world, like a web application or an API, you would use a `Load Balancer` service. For example, a public-facing ecommerce website running in Kubernetes could be exposed using a Load Balancer service.

From the manifest perspective, the only change you need to perform is exposing the service on a specific port such as 80/443 and setting the `service type as Load Balancer`.

```
apiVersion: v1
kind: Service
metadata:
  name: lb-svc
  labels:
    env: demo
spec:
```

53

```
type: Load Balancer
ports:
- port: 80
selector:
  env: demo
```

External Name

The last service type we have is ExternalName, which maps a Kubernetes service to a DNS name outside the cluster. Kubernetes does not assign an IP to the service; instead, it maps the CNAME record with the value of the external name specified.

```
apiVersion: v1
kind: Service
metadata:
  name: my-service
  namespace: prod
spec:
  type: ExternalName
  externalName: my.api.example.com
```

Role of Selectors in Service

Kubernetes services use label selectors to automatically discover and route traffic to the correct pods as the backend. When a service is created, it defines a selector that matches specific pod labels, ensuring that only those pods receive traffic.

For example, if a service has the below selector:

```
selector:
  env: demo
```

it will target all pods with the label env=demo as the backend to this service. This mapping ensures load balancing and fault tolerance, as pods can be added or removed without modifying the service.

Summary

- In Kubernetes, services enable applications running in pods to be accessible, ensuring seamless communication within the cluster or with external clients. Services act as load balancers, directing incoming requests to the appropriate backend pods.

- Kubernetes supports four service types:

    - **ClusterIP** (Default): Provides internal-only access within the Kubernetes cluster and is commonly used for multi-tier applications to enable communication between frontend, backend, and database tiers without external exposure.

    - **NodePort**: Exposes the service on a specific port (30000-32767) of each node, allowing external traffic via <NodeIP>:<NodePort>.

    - **Load Balancer**: Used for production applications to provision a cloud-managed external load balancer with a public IP and suitable for web applications and APIs needing external access. Please note that the Load Balancer service would default to NodePort behavior in environments without cloud-managed Kubernetes.

    - **ExternalName**: Maps a service to an external DNS name without assigning an internal IP and is ideal for connecting to external services outside the cluster.

CHAPTER 7

Namespaces

We have learned about different Kubernetes resources such as pods, deployments, services, etc., and how to manage them, but we have not discussed how to logically group them together for better management or isolate them (if needed).

Namespaces are Kubernetes objects that provide isolation of resources within the cluster. In Kubernetes, there are two types of resources:

- Namespace-scoped objects, such as pods, deployments, services, etc.

- Cluster-scoped objects, such as StorageClasses, nodes, PersistentVolumes, etc.

If you want to check what resources are namespace scoped and what are not, you can run the below commands:

```
# In a namespace
kubectl api-resources --namespaced=true
# Not in a namespace
kubectl api-resources --namespaced=false
```

When you create an object in Kubernetes, you can specify the namespace in which the object should be created; by default, the resources are created in the default namespace.

CHAPTER 7   NAMESPACES

When you create a new Kubernetes cluster, the following four namespaces are created along with it:

> **Default**: All the resources you create get created in this default namespace.
>
> **Kube-node-lease**: This namespace holds the lease object of each node that helps Kubelet to send heartbeats to the API Server to detect any node failure.
>
> **Kube-public**: This namespace is readable publicly without any authentication.
>
> **kube-system**: This namespace holds the Kubernetes-managed objects, including the control plane components.

Namespace Management

To create a namespace, you can apply the below sample YAML:

```
apiVersion: v1
kind: Namespace
metadata:
    name: mynamespace
```

or you can simply run the below imperative command which does the same thing:

```
kubectl create ns mynamespace
```

Note   You can use either the keyword namespace or ns.

CHAPTER 7 NAMESPACES

Now that we have familiarized ourselves with the kubectl utility, it's time to set the alias and bash completion to make our lives easy. You can execute the below commands:

```
source <(kubectl completion bash) # set up autocomplete in
bash into the current shell, bash-completion package should be
installed first.
echo "source <(kubectl completion bash)" >> ~/.bashrc # add
autocomplete permanently to your bash shell.
```

```
# set the alias
alias k=kubectl
complete -o default -F __start_kubectl k
```

Note You do not have to explicitly execute these commands on the exam sandbox as they will already be done for you.

To view the existing namespaces, simply run the below kubectl command:

```
kubectl get ns
```

Now, let's go back a few chapters, when we created our namespace-scoped resources such as pods, deployments, services, etc. We did not specify the namespace; hence, they were created in the `default` namespace.

What if we want to specify the namespace to be used?

We just have to pass the `--namespace mynamespace` parameter in the apply command or add the namespace field in the spec section of the resource. You can either use `--namespace namespacename` or `-n namespacename` in the kubectl command.

Figure 7-1 shows the terminal output of creating a deployment using the kubectl command with the namespace argument.

```
Piyush--->k create deploy nginx-demo --image=nginx -n demo
deployment.apps/nginx-demo created
```

Figure 7-1. *Pass the namespace flag in the kubectl command*

To access the resources from a particular namespace, you provide the --namespace or -n parameter along with the kubectl get command.

> **Note** We are using k instead of kubectl as we already set the alias.

Figure 7-2 shows the terminal output of how to get the deployment using the namespace argument.

```
Piyush--->k get deploy -n demo
NAME          READY   UP-TO-DATE   AVAILABLE   AGE
nginx-demo    1/1     1            1           17s
```

Figure 7-2. *Get deployment details for demo namespace*

> **Note** An important point to remember is that resources inside a namespace can communicate with each other with their hostname (service name); however, the resources from different namespaces do not have access to each other with their hostname but can only be accessed using an FQDN (Fully Qualified Domain Name).

Figure 7-3 shows that services within the same namespace can access each other via their name (hostname), but services in separate namespaces access each other via their FQDN.

CHAPTER 7 NAMESPACES

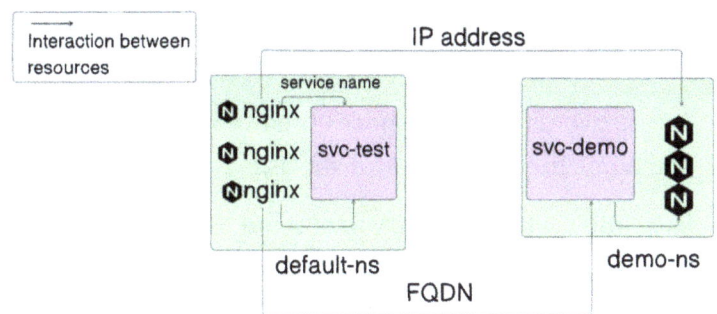

Figure 7-3. How services access each other across namespaces

Hostname is the service name on which a pod/deployment is exposed. FQDN name is the fully qualified name of the service and can be in the format

<service-name>.<namespacename>.svc.cluster.local

The above entry can also be obtained from the /etc/resolv.conf file on the pod.

To test this scenario, you can perform the below task:

- Create two namespaces and name them ns1 and ns2.

- Create a deployment with a single replica in each of these namespaces with the image as nginx and the names as deploy-ns1 and deploy-ns2, respectively.

- Get the IP address of each of the pods (remember the kubectl command for that?).

- Exec into the pod of deploy-ns1 and try to curl the IP address of the pod running on deploy-ns2.

- Your pod-to-pod connection should work, and you should be able to get a successful response back.

CHAPTER 7   NAMESPACES

- Now scale both of your deployments from one to three replicas.

- Create two services to expose both of your deployments and name them svc-ns1 and svc-ns2.

- Exec into each pod and try to curl the IP address of the service running on the other namespace.

- This curl should work.

- Now try doing the same using the service name instead of the IP. You will notice that you are getting an error saying "cannot resolve the host."

- Now use the FQDN of the service and try to curl again; this should work.

- In the end, delete both the namespaces, which should delete the services and deployments underneath them.

Summary

- Namespaces in Kubernetes provide isolation for resources within a cluster, enabling effective resource management and multi-tenancy.

- **Namespace-Scoped Resources**: Pods, deployments, services, etc.

- **Cluster-Wide Resources**: Nodes, PersistentVolumes, StorageClasses, etc.

- By default, resources are created in the default namespace unless specified otherwise. A new Kubernetes cluster initializes with four predefined namespaces:

  - **Default**: Default namespace for user-created resources
  - **Kube-node-lease**: Contains node lease objects for Kubelet heartbeats
  - **Kube-public**: Publicly readable namespace without authentication
  - **Kube-system**: Stores Kubernetes-managed objects and control plane components

- **Within a Namespace**: Resources can communicate using their hostname (e.g., service name).

- **Across Namespaces**: Resources require a Fully Qualified Domain Name (FQDN) in the format

  `<service-name>.<namespace>.svc.cluster.local`

- By organizing resources with namespaces, Kubernetes ensures better isolation, resource management, and scalability.

CHAPTER 8

DaemonSet, CronJob, and Job

Now that we know about the fundamental Kubernetes resources and how to manage them, it's time we look into more advanced resources that can be deployed for various purposes. Resources such as DaemonSet, CronJob, and jobs will be covered in this chapter.

DaemonSet

DaemonSet is a Kubernetes resource that ensures that an identical replica is deployed to each of the available nodes in the cluster.

This is different from deployment in many ways. In deployment, we specify the number of replicas in the manifest file as the desired number of replicas we need irrespective of the number of nodes in the cluster; however, DaemonSet deploys one replica to each of the available nodes except the node that is tainted (we will cover the concept of taints and toleration later in the book).

This is useful for many use cases, such as monitoring agents, logging agents, networking CNIs (Container Network Interfaces), etc., in which we need to process or gather some information from each of the running nodes.

CHAPTER 8   DAEMONSET, CRONJOB, AND JOB

You don't need to update the replica based on demand; the DaemonSet takes care of it by spinning X number of pods for X number of nodes. If you create a DaemonSet in a cluster of five nodes, then five pods will be created by default. If you add another node to the cluster, a new pod will be automatically created on the new node.

Figure 8-1 shows the architectural diagram and hierarchy of a sample DaemonSet (kube-proxy) inside a Kubernetes cluster.

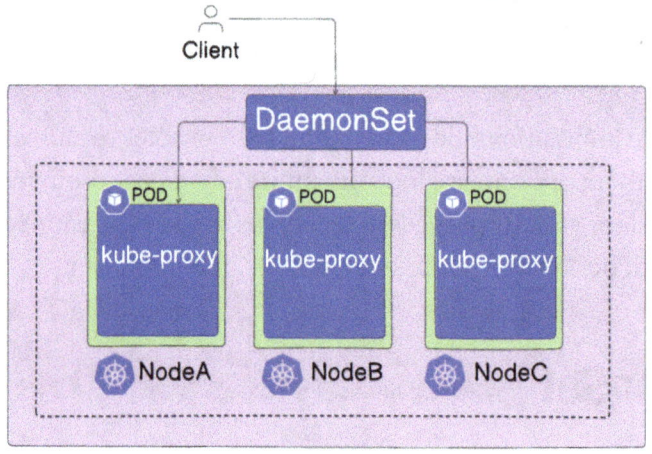

Figure 8-1. *DaemonSet in Kubernetes*

The manifest file of a DaemonSet is similar to a deployment manifest with a slight change of `Kind: DaemonSet` instead of `Kind: Deployment`, and you do not need to specify the replicas field in DaemonSet.

```
apiVersion: apps/v1
kind:  DaemonSet
metadata:
  name: nginx-ds
  labels:
    env: demo
```

```
spec:
  template:
    metadata:
      labels:
        env: demo
      name: nginx
    spec:
      containers:
      - image: nginx
        name: nginx
        ports:
        - containerPort: 80
  selector:
    matchLabels:
      env: demo
```

Job

A job is a type of Kubernetes object that creates one or more pods to perform a task. Once the tasks are completed, the pods are marked as completed, and the job tracks the successful completion of the task. Deleting a job will clean up the pods that it created.

To create a job, we can use the below sample manifest that can be used for a data processing pipeline:

```
apiVersion: batch/v1
  kind: Job
  metadata:
    name: data-processor-job
    spec:
      template:
```

```
      spec:
      containers:
      - name: processor
        image: python:3.9-slim
        command:
        - python
        - -c
        - |
        import time
        print('processing data...')
        time.sleep(10)
        print('data processing completed..')
      restartPolicy: Never
    backoffLimit: 2
```

Key components

- **backoffLimit**: Number of retries before a job fails (two attempts).

- **restartPolicy: Never**: The pod won't restart on failure.

CronJob

CronJob is a type of Kubernetes object that creates one or more scheduled jobs based on the cron syntax. CronJobs are meant to perform regular scheduled tasks such as backup, report generation, data processing, etc.

```
apiVersion: batch/v1
kind: CronJob
metadata:
  name: print-40daysofkubernetes
```

```
spec:
  schedule: "*/5 * * * *"
  jobTemplate:
    spec:
      template:
        spec:
          containers:
          - name: printer
            image: busybox
            command:
            - /bin/sh
            - -c
            - "echo '#40daysofkubernetes'"
          restartPolicy: OnFailure
```

CronJob prints #40daysofkubernetes every five minutes.

Summary

- **DaemonSet** ensures a replica is deployed on each node in the cluster. Unlike deployments, which require a specified number of replicas, DaemonSets automatically create one pod per node except tainted nodes (the concept of taints and tolerations will be covered later in the book).

- Use cases for DaemonSets include monitoring agents, logging agents, networking CNIs, and any task requiring data collection or processing on all nodes.

CHAPTER 8   DAEMONSET, CRONJOB, AND JOB

- A **job** creates one or more pods to perform a specific task and ensures completion. Once the task finishes, the pods are marked as completed, and deleting the job removes all associated pods. Jobs are suitable for tasks like data processing pipelines or something that can be triggered on an ad hoc basis.

- **CronJob** schedules and runs jobs at specified intervals using cron syntax. Common use cases include regular backups, report generation, and periodic data processing.

CHAPTER 9

Static Pods and Scheduling

In addition to learning about Kubernetes components, we have also studied pods, which are the smallest deployable unit. However, how are these control plane components configured in the cluster and managed? We will discuss static pods and scheduling in this chapter.

Static Pods

Static pods are a special type of pod in Kubernetes that are managed directly by Kubelet on each node rather than the Kube-Scheduler. Manifest files of static pods are placed directly on the node's file system at a particular directory; for example, /etc/kubernetes/manifest is the default directory where the Kubelet watches these files.

Some examples of static pods are control plane components such as **API Server**, **Kube-Scheduler**, **Controller Manager**, **ETCD**, etc. If you remove the manifest file(s) from the directory, that pod will be deleted from the cluster.

If you are still using the KinD cluster that we have created earlier, then you can do a docker exec in the control plane node and check the manifests in the /etc/kubernetes/manifests folder:

```
docker exec -it cka-cluster-control-plane bash
```

You might be wondering why we are doing a docker exec. If you remember, nodes in our KinD cluster are nothing but the containers, and to enter into a container, we use the docker exec command.

To restart a component such as kube-scheduler, you can move the kube-scheduler manifest to a different directory, and you will see the kube-scheduler is not running anymore, which means new pods will not be assigned to the nodes. Newly created pods will be stuck in a pending state as the scheduler is down.

As soon as you move the manifest back to its original directory, the scheduler pod will start, and the pending workload pod will be created.

Manual Scheduling

Kube-scheduler is not the only way for scheduling a pod. You can also do manual scheduling by specifying the nodeName field in the spec section of the pod manifest. This is not a recommended approach, but it is possible to do that in case you are troubleshooting some issue for a particular node.

```
apiVersion: v1
kind: Pod
metadata:
   name: nginx-pod
spec:
   containers:
   - name: nginx
     image: nginx:latest
   nodeName: cka-cluster-worker-1
```

If the pod spec already has this field (nodeName), then the scheduler will not pick that pod for scheduling; the pod will be scheduled on the particular node irrespective of the scheduler health status.

CHAPTER 9   STATIC PODS AND SCHEDULING

Labels and Selectors

Labels are the key-value pairs attached to Kubernetes objects like pods, services, and deployments. They help organize and group resources based on the specific criteria.

For example, you can use the environment, type, tier, and application labels in the below sample pod:

```
apiVersion: v1
kind: Pod
metadata:
   name: nginx-pod
   labels:
      environment: production
      type: frontend
      tier: web
      application: my-app
spec:
   containers:
   - name: nginx
     image: nginx:latest
     ports:
     - containerPort: 80
```

As you can see, the labels are part of metadata; hence, no impact on the actual application. You can check the labels using the below command:

```
kubectl get pods –show-labels
```

Selectors can be used to filter Kubernetes objects based on their **labels**. This is helpful for querying and managing a subset of objects that meet specific criteria. For instance, if you want to filter all of the frontend pods, you can use the below command:

```
kubectl get pods --selector tier=frontend
```

CHAPTER 9   STATIC PODS AND SCHEDULING

Annotations are similar to labels but attach non-identifying metadata to objects, for example, recording the release version of an application for information purposes or last applied configuration details, etc.

Taints and Tolerations

Taints are like putting up fences on the node(s), and only a certain type of pods has access to be scheduled on those node. A taint marks a node with specific characteristics, such as gpu=true. By default, pods cannot be scheduled on that tainted node unless they have a special permission called toleration. When a toleration on a pod matches with the taint on the node, then only the pod will be scheduled on that node.

Let's look at that with the help of an example.

You can taint a node by specifying the taint in the format

```
key=value:effect
kubectl taint nodes node1 key=gpu:NoSchedule
```

This command taints node1 with the key "gpu" and the effect "NoSchedule." Pods without a toleration for this taint won't be scheduled there.

Toleration can be added in the pod in the spec section of the manifest with key, operator, value, and effect fields, which should match the taint on the node:

```
apiVersion: v1
kind: Pod
metadata:
  labels:
    run: redis
  name: redis
spec:
  containers:
```

```
  - image: redis
    name: redis
  tolerations:
  - key: "gpu"
    operator: "Equal"
    value: "true"
    effect: "NoSchedule"
```

This pod specification defines a toleration for the "gpu" taint with the effect "NoSchedule." This allows the pod to be scheduled on tainted nodes.

To remove the taint on the node, you can add a - at the end of the taint command:

```
kubectl taint nodes node1 key=gpu:NoSchedule-
```

> **Note** Labels group nodes based on size, type, environment, etc. Unlike taints, labels don't directly affect scheduling but are useful for organizing resources.

Another important point to remember is that taints and tolerations only restrict what type of workloads are allowed to a particular node, but that does not guarantee the scheduling of a particular pod on a specific node.

For example, there are two nodes, node1 and node2, and node1 is tainted with gpu=true, and we have created a pod named nginx with the toleration gpu=true. Node1 will only accept the nginx pod or any other pod that has the same toleration, but the nginx pod can also be scheduled on Node2, as the node is not tainted and can accept the pod based on other constraints such as resource requests and limits, capacity, affinity, and so on (we will look at these concepts later in the book).

Node Affinity

You can use the nodeSelector field in your pod manifest to schedule a pod on a node with the labels provided in the selector field; however, if you need more control over the scheduling, in which you can indicate whether the rule is soft or preferred, you can use NodeAffinity in that case.

Node affinity lets you define the rules for your pods to be scheduled on a particular type of node based on the node labels. Taints provide the capability of a node to accept certain types of pods. Node affinity works similarly, but it provides the capabilities to the pods to go on a particular type of node for scheduling (the other way around).

There are two main properties in node affinity:

- **requiredDuringSchedulingIgnoredDuringExecution**: The scheduler can't schedule the pod unless the rule is met.

- **preferredDuringSchedulingIgnoredDuringExecution**: The scheduler will try to schedule the pod on a node that meets the rule. If a matching node is not available, the scheduler will still schedule the pod.

Here's how it works: you define a list of required node labels in your pod spec, for example, disktype=ssd. Based on that, the scheduler tries to place the pod on the nodes with those exact labels; once scheduled, the pod remains on the node even if the label changes.

Below is the sample node affinity:

```
apiVersion: v1
kind: Pod
metadata:
  creationTimestamp: null
  labels:
    run: redis
  name: redis-3
```

CHAPTER 9 STATIC PODS AND SCHEDULING

```
spec:
  containers:
  - image: redis
    name: redis
    resources: {}
  dnsPolicy: ClusterFirst
  restartPolicy: Always
  affinity:
    nodeAffinity:
  requiredDuringSchedulingIgnoredDuringExecution:
        nodeSelectorTerms:
        - matchExpressions:
          - key: disktype
            operator: In
            values:
            - ssd
```

Resource Requests and Limits

In your Kubernetes cluster, each pod requires a certain amount of resources, such as memory, CPU, GPU, etc., to function properly. Kubernetes allows you to define how much resources are required by a particular workload to operate normally (requests) and how much is the maximum it can use (limits).

It has many benefits:

> **Scheduling Decisions**: Based on the specified requests and limits, the scheduler can take the decision whether a node has enough capacity to schedule that workload.

77

Node Safeguarding: If a container tries to use more resources than the limits, Kubernetes will perform CPU throttling; in the case of memory, it will kill the container with an OOM error (out of memory) to prevent the overconsumption of memory from the node that could result in node failure as well.

Minimize the Blast Radius: Limit protects your workloads from resource exhaustion by preventing a single container from occupying the resources that could have been used by other workloads.

For example, a pod requesting more memory than is available will be killed due to an OOM (out of memory) error.

```
apiVersion: v1
kind: Pod
metadata:
  name: memory-demo-2
  namespace: mem-example
spec:
  containers:
  - name: memory-demo-2-ctr
    image: polinux/stress
    resources:
      requests:
        memory: "50Mi"
      limits:
        memory: "100Mi"
    command: ["stress"]
    args: ["--vm", "1", "--vm-bytes", "250M", "--vm-hang", "1"]
```

The below pod will be scheduled:

```
apiVersion: v1
kind: Pod
metadata:
  name: memory-demo
  namespace: mem-example
spec:
  containers:
  - name: memory-demo-ctr
    image: polinux/stress
    resources:
      requests:
        memory: "100Mi"
      limits:
        memory: "200Mi"
    command: ["stress"]
    args: ["--vm", "1", "--vm-bytes", "150M", "--vm-hang", "1"]
```

configmap and Secrets

Using the same values in multiple places inside the manifest YAMLs is a tedious and inefficient task; hence, Kubernetes provides an object called configmaps, using which you can take out similar environment variables from the manifest and store them in a separate object in the key-value pair. You can then inject the configmap into one or more pods instead of writing the same variables again and again.

Here's a sample command to create the configmap:

```
kubectl create cm <configmapname> \ --from-literal=firstname=piyush
```

CHAPTER 9　STATIC PODS AND SCHEDULING

Or, you can use the below sample manifest YAML (declarative way):

```
apiVersion: v1
data:
  firstname: piyush
  lastname: sachdeva
kind: configmap
metadata:
  name: app-cm
```

Once created, you can use the configmap as below:

```
apiVersion: v1
kind: Pod
metadata:
  name: myapp-pod
  labels:
    app.kubernetes.io/name: MyApp
spec:
  containers:
  - name: myapp-container
    image: busybox:1.28
    env:
    - name: FIRSTNAME
      valueFrom:
        configMapKeyRef:
          name: app-cm
          key: firstname
    command: ['sh', '-c', 'echo The app is running! && sleep 3600']
```

CHAPTER 9   STATIC PODS AND SCHEDULING

However, if you noticed, we have given the environment variable reference from the configmap; this could be an inefficient task if there are many environment variables inside the configmap. To avoid that, we can give the reference of the entire configmap as below:

```
envFrom:
- configMapRef:
    name: app-cm
```

Secrets

Secrets are similar to configmaps but are specifically intended to hold confidential data. Secrets in Kubernetes are by default base64 encoded, not encrypted, meaning you can decode the secrets without needing any private key or certificate.

Secrets can contain sensitive data such as passwords, tokens, or an SSH key. It is recommended to keep the sensitive data away from the pod specification in a separate object, such as a secret, which can be used inside the pod by providing the reference to the secret object or mounting the secret as a volume on the pod.

Different types of secrets supported by Kubernetes:

- **Opaque Secrets**: User-defined data in a key-value pair
- **Docker Registry Secrets**: Docker credentials to pull images from Docker registries
- **Basic Auth**: Secrets in the form of username and password
- **ssh-auth**: SSH authentication secret
- **TLS**: Data for a TLS client and server
- **Kubernetes Token**: Bootstrap token data

81

Opaque is the default secret type if you don't explicitly specify a type in a secret manifest.

To create an opaque secret, you can use the below command:

```
kubectl create secret generic <secret-name> --from-literal=password=<your-password>
```

or the below declarative YAML:

```yaml
apiVersion: v1
kind: Pod
metadata:
  name: sample-pod
spec:
  containers:
  - name: nginx
    image: nginx
    env:
    - name: PASSWORD
      valueFrom:
        secretKeyRef:
          name: demo-secret
          key: password
```

To create a docker-registry secret, you can use this command:

```
kubectl create secret docker-registry sample-docker-secret \
--docker-email=sample@example.com \ --docker-username=scott \
--docker-password=tiger \   --docker-server=my-registry.example:5000
```

The above command creates a secret of type kubernetes.io/dockerconfigjson. You can then retrieve the data from the secret and decode it using base64, as the secret will be stored as a base64-encoded string.

CHAPTER 9 STATIC PODS AND SCHEDULING

Summary

- **Static pods** are managed directly by the Kubelet on each node rather than the Kubernetes Scheduler. Their manifest files are placed on the node's file system, typically in /etc/kubernetes/manifests, where the Kubelet continuously monitors them.
- Examples of static pods include control plane components such as API Server, Kube-Scheduler, Controller Manager, and ETCD.
- Removing a manifest file from this directory deletes the corresponding pod from the cluster.
- You can restart static pods by moving their manifest files out of the monitored directory and back.
- Manual scheduling bypasses the Kubernetes Scheduler by specifying the nodeName field in the pod's manifest.
- While manual scheduling is not recommended for regular use, it is helpful for troubleshooting specific nodes or in case of a custom scheduler.
- Labels and selectors facilitate organizing and filtering Kubernetes resources. Labels, defined as key-value pairs, are added to metadata and do not impact the application.
- Selectors use these labels to query or manage subsets of resources, while annotations provide non-identifying metadata for informational purposes, such as versioning or configuration details.

CHAPTER 9   STATIC PODS AND SCHEDULING

- Taints and tolerations control which pods can be scheduled on specific nodes.

- A taint, defined as key=value:effect, prevents pods without matching tolerations from being scheduled on a node.

- Taints and tolerations only restrict unsuitable pods but do not guarantee placement on a specific node.

- Node affinity enables more granular control over scheduling using node labels. Rules can be strict (requiredDuringSchedulingIgnoredDuringExecution) or flexible (preferredDuringSchedulingIgnoredDuringExecution). For example, a pod with disktype=ssd required affinity will only schedule on nodes with that label. Node affinity complements taints and tolerations by enabling pods to select preferred nodes.

- Resource requests and limits define the minimum and maximum resources a pod can use, such as CPU, memory, or GPU.

- Properly configured requests and limits protect against resource exhaustion and optimize cluster performance.

- configmaps and secrets manage application configuration and sensitive data, respectively.

- configmaps store non-confidential key-value pairs for reuse across manifests, simplifying management.

- Secrets store sensitive data like passwords or tokens, encoded in base64 to be injected into pods.

- Kubernetes supports various secret types, including opaque (default), docker-registry credentials, and TLS data.

- Secrets can be injected into pods as environment variables or mounted as volumes, keeping sensitive information separate from pod specifications.

CHAPTER 10

Autoscaling in Kubernetes

Imagine you are an ecommerce enterprise and hosted your main web application on Kubernetes. You have 20 nodes running as per your predicted traffic during an event such as Black Friday or Cyber Monday; however, your traffic spike was 20 times more than you predicted. What could happen at that time?

Your workload starts failing, with business impact, user impact, revenue loss, goodwill impact, and so on.

You can try to add more nodes to the cluster during peak hours. But can you keep doing it throughout the event and during the next event and so on?

Also, it is not effective and requires huge manpower to execute those tasks seamlessly. These are one of the situations when we can use autoscaling, which adds more resources (CPU, memory, nodes, etc.) automatically as per the traffic requirements.

Autoscaling also helps in cost optimization by deleting extra resources when traffic utilization comes back to normal (off-peak hours).

CHAPTER 10   AUTOSCALING IN KUBERNETES

There are different types of scaling in Kubernetes, broadly categorized into

- **Horizontal Scaling**: Automatically adding/deleting resources to the existing infra (scale out/scale in)
- **Vertical Scaling**: Automatically resize the server to a bigger/smaller size (scale up/scale down)

Figure 10-1 shows the different autoscaling options available in Kubernetes.

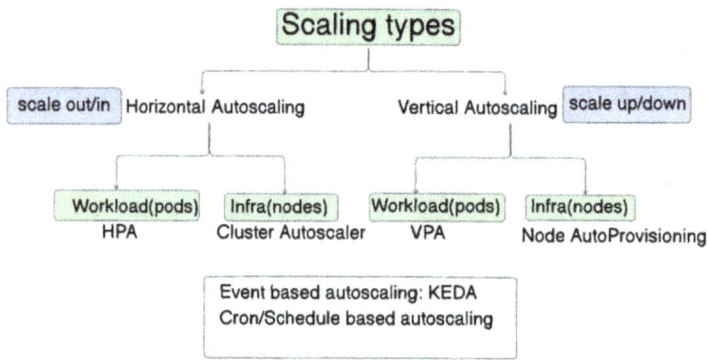

Figure 10-1. *Autoscaling types in Kubernetes*

HPA (Horizontal Pod Autoscaling)

HPA is a concept derived from horizontal scaling, which is when more pods are being added when the traffic increases (scale out) and pods are being deleted when traffic goes down (scale in). HPA is helpful when you can't afford application downtime during the scaling; adding more pods would not impact the existing application.

Figure 10-2 shows how horizontal pod autoscaling works in Kubernetes.

CHAPTER 10   AUTOSCALING IN KUBERNETES

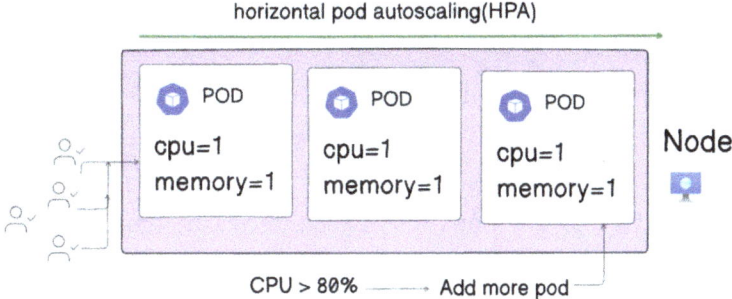

Figure 10-2. Horizontal pod autoscaling (HPA) example

VPA (Vertical Pod Autoscaling)

VPA is a concept derived from vertical scaling in which a bigger pod (more CPU/memory) would be automatically added and replace the existing pod (scale up). Once the traffic comes back to normal, the bigger pod is again replaced by a small pod (scale down). VPA is useful in cases when you can afford some disruption, even though the disruption would be minimal if you are rolling out changes in a rolling update or blue-green approach.

Figure 10-3 shows how vertical pod autoscaling works in Kubernetes.

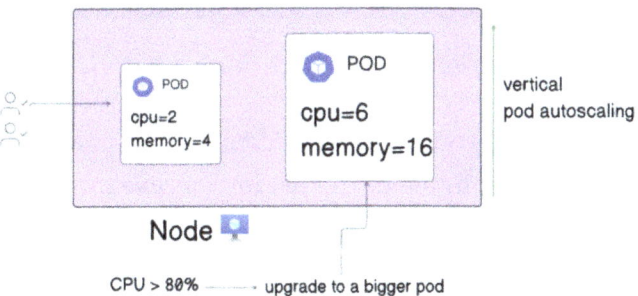

Figure 10-3. Vertical pod autoscaling example

CHAPTER 10 AUTOSCALING IN KUBERNETES

Metrics Server

The Metrics Server is an application that runs as a deployment on your Kubernetes cluster and helps collect the resource metrics from Kubelet. These metrics are then exposed to the Kubernetes API Server through the Metrics API. HPA and VPA consume these metrics and take the autoscaling decision.

To deploy the Metrics Server, you can follow the instructions given on the GitHub project: https://github.com/kubernetes-sigs/metrics-server.

Once the Metrics Server is deployed, you can test if the Metrics API is being exposed by running the below command, which shows the metrics like CPU limits and usage and memory limits and usage, respectively:

```
kubectl top pods
kubectl top nodes
```

Figure 10-4 shows the terminal output of the top node command.

```
Piyush—>k top node
NAME                       CPU(cores)   CPU%   MEMORY(bytes)   MEMORY%
cka-cluster3-control-plane 415m         5%     753Mi           19%
cka-cluster3-worker        72m          0%     194Mi           4%
cka-cluster3-worker2       90m          1%     226Mi           5%
```

Figure 10-4. *CPU and memory utilizations per node*

To implement HPA, you can create a deployment object and autoscale it using an imperative command with parameters like threshold for HPA, minimum pods, and maximum pods for autoscaling:

```
kubectl autoscale deployment php-apache \ --cpu-percent=50 --min=1 --max=10
```

Figure 10-5 shows the terminal output of configuring HPA on the cluster based on CPU utilization.

CHAPTER 10 AUTOSCALING IN KUBERNETES

```
Piyush—>k autoscale deploy php-apache --cpu-percent=50 --min=1 --max=10
horizontalpodautoscaler.autoscaling/php-apache autoscaled
Piyush—>k get hpa
NAME         REFERENCE              TARGETS            MINPODS  MAXPODS  REPLICAS  AGE
php-apache   Deployment/php-apache  cpu: <unknown>/50% 1        10       0         8s
Piyush—>k get hpa
NAME         REFERENCE              TARGETS            MINPODS  MAXPODS  REPLICAS  AGE
php-apache   Deployment/php-apache  cpu: 1%/50%        1        10       1         30s
Piyush—>
```

Figure 10-5. HPA setup using the kubectl command

To test the HPA, you can simulate load on the application by using a load generator as below:

kubectl run -i --tty load-generator --rm \ --image=busybox:1.28 --restart=Never -- /bin/sh -c \ "while sleep 0.01; do wget -q -O- \ http://php-apache; done"

The above command will keep performing wget on the application's pod every few microseconds, resulting in increasing the load on the application.

Once you have done that, you can run the command kubectl get hpa -watch, and you can see the CPU utilization has drastically increased after a few minutes, which breached the threshold of 50% CPU utilization and added more pods to the deployment php-apache.

Figure 10-6 shows the terminal output of autoscaling in real time using the --watch argument to the kubectl command.

```
Piyush—>k get hpa --watch
NAME         REFERENCE              TARGETS       MINPODS  MAXPODS  REPLICAS  AGE
php-apache   Deployment/php-apache  cpu: 167%/50% 1        10       1         3m27s
^CPiyush—>k get po
NAME                          READY  STATUS   RESTARTS  AGE
load-generator                1/1    Running  0         46s
php-apache-678865dd57-cpctl   1/1    Running  0         15s
php-apache-678865dd57-dx582   1/1    Running  0         6m9s
php-apache-678865dd57-h8lnr   1/1    Running  0         15s
php-apache-678865dd57-v9smf   0/1    Pending  0         0s
php-apache-678865dd57-zcmbq   1/1    Running  0         15s
Piyush—>
```

Figure 10-6. HPA in real time using --watch

You can also create the HPA object using the YAML provided:

```yaml
apiVersion: autoscaling/v2
kind: HorizontalPodAutoscaler
metadata:
  name: php-apache
spec:
  scaleTargetRef:
    apiVersion: apps/v1
    kind: Deployment
    name: php-apache
  minReplicas: 1
  maxReplicas: 10
  metrics:
  - type: Resource
    resource:
      name: cpu
      target:
        type: Utilization
        averageUtilization: 50
```

Now, you can delete the load-generator pod, and you will see the newly added pods in terminating state till they reached the minimum number of replicas which is one.

Cluster Autoscaling

Cluster autoscaler provides similar functionalities of HPA and VPA, but instead of autoscaling your pods, it does the autoscaling of your nodes. The Kubernetes Add-On Cluster Autoscaler adds or deletes new nodes for horizontal node autoscaling; it also upgrades the node to a bigger size for vertical node autoscaling.

CHAPTER 10   AUTOSCALING IN KUBERNETES

It automatically manages the nodes in your cluster as per the traffic.

NAP (Node Auto-provisioning)

The feature of NAP mostly comes with a managed cloud service such as AKS, EKS, GKE, etc., in which new node pools (collection of similar types of nodes based on their resource requirement, size, machine type, etc.) are being added/deleted as per the demand.

Liveness vs. Readiness vs. Startup Probes

How would Kubelet know when to restart an application, when an application is unhealthy, or when to add more pods to replace the unhealthy pods?

It does that by probing the application. This is referred to as health probes, in which the Kubelet keeps checking the application after a certain period and reports if it is healthy or not; based on that, it takes certain actions to recover from the failure.

There are three types of health probes in Kubernetes:

- **Readiness Probe**: Ensures that your application is healthy

- **Liveness Probe**: Restarts the application if the health check fails

- **Startup Probe**: Probes for legacy applications that need a lot of time to start

Figure 10-7 shows the different health probes available in Kubernetes.

Chapter 10 Autoscaling in Kubernetes

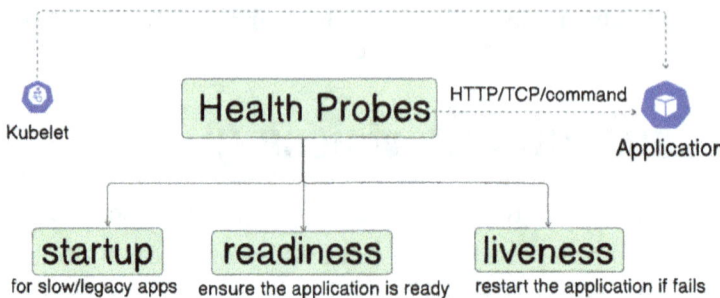

Figure 10-7. Health probes in Kubernetes

Readiness Probe: The readiness probe is used to determine if a container is ready to start accepting traffic. If the readiness probe fails, Kubernetes will temporarily remove the pod from the service's load balancers, and it won't receive any traffic until it passes the readiness check again.

We normally use readiness probes to prevent traffic from being routed to containers that are not yet ready to serve requests (during startup, initialization, or maintenance).

Types of readiness probes:

- HTTP request
- TCP probe
- Readiness command

To create a sample HTTP request-based probe, you can use the below YAML with the readinessProbe field inside the container section, meaning the probes are applied at the container level instead of the pod level:

```
apiVersion: v1
kind: Pod
metadata:
  name: hello
```

```
spec:
  containers:
  - name: readiness
    image: registry.k8s.io/e2e-test-images/agnhost:2.40
    readinessProbe:
      httpGet:
        path: /healthz
        port: 8080
      initialDelaySeconds: 15
      periodSeconds: 10
```

The YAML above demonstrates the readiness probe of type HTTP request, which uses port 8080 to probe the readiness container on path /healthz every 10 seconds (periodSeconds). However, it will wait 15 seconds (initialDelaySeconds) before beginning the probe.

Liveness Probes: The liveness probe is used to determine if a container is running. If the liveness probe fails, Kubernetes will kill the container, and it will be restarted according to the pod's restart policy. It ensures that unhealthy containers are being terminated and replaced with healthy containers to maintain high availability and self-healing of the application.

Types of liveness probes:

- HTTP request
- TCP probe
- Command based
- gRPC probe

CHAPTER 10   AUTOSCALING IN KUBERNETES

Liveness command-based probe sample:

```yaml
apiVersion: v1
kind: Pod
metadata:
  labels:
    test: liveness
  name: liveness-exec
spec:
  containers:
  - name: liveness
    image: registry.k8s.io/busybox
    args:
    - /bin/sh
    - -c
    - touch /tmp/healthy; sleep 30; rm -f /tmp/healthy;
      sleep 600
    livenessProbe:
      exec:
        command:
        - cat
        - /tmp/healthy
      initialDelaySeconds: 5
      periodSeconds: 5
```

The YAML above demonstrates the liveness probe of type command, which uses the command car /tmp/healthy to probe the `liveness` container every five seconds (periodSeconds). However, it will wait five seconds (initialDelaySeconds) before beginning the probe. In simple words, it is checking the presence of the file (/tmp/healthy) and ensuring that the container is healthy when the file is present.

CHAPTER 10   AUTOSCALING IN KUBERNETES

Summary

- Autoscaling in Kubernetes ensures resource scalability and cost optimization by dynamically adjusting infrastructure based on traffic requirements. This eliminates manual intervention during unexpected traffic surges, such as during Black Friday events, and prevents business impact from application failures.

- **Horizontal Scaling**: Adds or removes pods or nodes (scale out/in) to handle fluctuating traffic.

- You should deploy Metrics Server to collect and expose resource metrics for HPA and VPA.

- **Vertical Scaling**: Adjusts pod or node resources (scales up/down) to meet demand.

- **Cluster Autoscaling**: Manages node-level scaling, adding or upgrading nodes automatically to meet demand. The cluster autoscaler is often used with cloud-managed services like EKS, AKS, and GKE.

- **Node Auto-provisioning (NAP)**: Automatically adds or deletes node pools based on traffic requirements.

- Kubernetes uses health probes to maintain high availability and self-healing by monitoring application health.

- **Readiness Probe**: Checks if a container is ready to receive traffic. It temporarily removes unhealthy containers from load balancers until they recover.

- **Liveness Probe**: Ensures a container is running. If a probe fails, the container is restarted by the probe, based on the pod's restart policy.

- **Startup Probe**: Used for legacy applications with long initialization times, ensuring readiness before traffic routing.

CHAPTER 11

Manifest Management Tools

In this chapter, we will explore Kubernetes manifest management tools—**Helm** and **Kustomize**—which simplify and streamline the deployment of complex applications. We will learn how Helm uses templating and charts to package, configure, and version Kubernetes resources, making it ideal for managing reusable and shareable application definitions. Kustomize, on the other hand, takes a patch-based, declarative approach that enables you to customize YAML manifests without duplication.

Helm

Helm is a package manager for Kubernetes, just like we have apt for Ubuntu, yum for Red Hat, and so on. When you have to install a package in Ubuntu, you go to the package manager repository and install the package using that. A package manager provides an easy way to install and manage software packages.

In Kubernetes, Helm provides similar functionality; for example, if you want to install Prometheus, you can just install it using Helm instead of going to the Prometheus website and downloading its binaries or installables. Helm is also a CNCF (Cloud Native Community Foundation) project that provides you with fantastic community support.

Helm has three main components:

- **Helm Chart**: A package in Helm is called a chart or a Helm chart, like an RPM file or a dpkg file. It's a bundle of tools, binaries, and dependencies with multiple deployment manifests.
- **Repository**: A central storage for chart management like Docker Hub.
- **Release**: An instance of a running chart; for example, we have containers in Docker, which is a running instance of a Docker image.

Charts are reusable, and you can install a single chart multiple times, and each time it will create a new release. You can also search Helm charts in the Kubernetes repository.

Getting Started with Helm

To create a sample Helm chart, you can use the command

```
helm create <chartname>
```

It will create the following directory structure:

```
|-- .helmignore
|-- chart.yaml   # metadata about the chart
|-- values.yaml # override the values in template files
|-- charts/   # chart dependency
|-- template/   # Template files
        └── /tests/
```

The template file will look something like

```
apiVersion: v1
kind: Service
```

```
metadata:
  name: {{ .Values.serviceName }}
spec:
  type: {{ .Values.serviceType }}
  ports:
  - port: 80
    selector:
      app: acs-helloworld-{{.Release.Name}}
```

in which you have defined certain variables such as serviceName, serviceType, ReleaseName, etc. These values come from a file called values.yaml and from the release metadata inside chart.yaml. Here's the content stored in values.yaml in a key-value format:

```
serviceName: helloworld
serviceType: ClusterIP
```

Here's the content from chart.yaml:

```
apiVersion: v1
description: A Helm chart for Kubernetes
name: helloworld
version: 0.1.1
```

You can update values.yaml as per your needs, and you can use the single chart for multiple environments, and each time it will create a new release. You can also pass the custom values.yaml for each environment.

To install an existing chart, you can add the repo and install using the command

```
helm repo add azure-samples \ https://azure-samples.github.io/helm-charts/
```

```
helm install azure-samples/aks-helloworld --set crds.enabled=true
```

CHAPTER 11   MANIFEST MANAGEMENT TOOLS

Kustomize

In the previous topic, we learned about the package manager for Kubernetes (Helm) and understood how it uses templating for simplified management of your Kubernetes and bundles all the files into something known as a Helm chart. Kustomize is a similar tool; however, it provides additional functionalities such as managing and organizing application configurations across different environments without using the templating engine functionality of Helm.

Kustomize takes a fundamentally different approach to configuration management compared to other tools like Helm. Instead of using templates and variables, it uses a layered approach that builds upon your existing YAML manifests. This makes it particularly appealing for beginners as it requires minimal learning of new concepts while providing powerful customization capabilities.

Helm uses a declarative approach in which you can define a base configuration (common configuration) that can be used for all the environments and separate configuration (overlays) that you can define for each of the environments, providing you capabilities to make changes for each of the environments without changing the common configuration. You can keep your common changes (that need to be applied for all the manifests, such as common tags, common environment variables, etc.) and keep the environment-specific configuration in their dedicated directories (such as environment name, labels, resource requests, limits, etc.).

Getting Started with Kustomize

What makes Kustomize particularly accessible is its integration with kubectl. You don't need to install additional tools—it's already there, within the kubectl utility.

CHAPTER 11   MANIFEST MANAGEMENT TOOLS

You start a simple `kustomization.yaml` file, which acts as your main configuration file.

Consider a typical application setup with a deployment, service, and configmap. To kustomize it, you start by creating a new file in the root directory of your project and call it `kustomization.yaml`. Then move the common labels, prefixes/suffixes, and annotations from each of the manifest files to the below kustomization.yaml file:

```
resources:
  - deployment.yaml
  - service.yaml
  - configmap.yaml
commonLabels:
  app: mydemoapp
commonAnnotations:
  app: myanno
namePrefix: kustom-
nameSuffix: -v0.1
```

In the above sample kustomization.yaml, we have five top-level fields:

- **resources**: You can define all your manifest YAMLs here.

- **commonLabels**: The common labels that you wish to be applied to all the resources.

- **commonAnnotations**: The common annotations that you wish to be applied to all the resources.

- **namePrefix**: A valid prefix that will be applied to the resource's name.

- **nameSuffix**: A valid suffix that will be applied to the resource's name.

Once you have created your kustomization.yaml, you can execute the command

`kubectl kustomize .`

It will generate a manifest YAML by overriding all the fields in existing YAMLs; you can apply the changes by redirecting to a file such as

```
kubectl kustomize . > manifest.yaml
kubectl apply -f manifest.yaml
```

or you can also run

`kubectl apply -k .`

where -k stands for Kustomize. To apply any manifest to the Kubernetes cluster, we used kubectl apply -f <filename>; there is a slight difference while applying the kustomize manifest; it looks for the file customization.yaml in the current directory as we have used a dot (.).

configmap Generator

Kustomize also provides you the capabilities of generating configmaps from external files, which allows you to separate Kubernetes configuration data from Kubernetes manifests as per best practices.

You achieve this by following the below steps:

1. Add the below field in the kustomization.yaml:

    ```
    configMapGenerator:
    - name: <mapname>
        env: config.properties
    ```

2. Update the reference of the configmap name inside the manifest YAML.

CHAPTER 11　MANIFEST MANAGEMENT TOOLS

Managing Multiple Environments

The true strength of Kustomize shines in managing multiple environments. By organizing your configurations into base and overlay directories, you create a clear hierarchy of configurations.

Earlier, you had everything inside a root directory, for example:

```
$HOME/
    ├── deployment.yaml
    ├── service.yaml
    ├── config.properties
    └── kustomization.yaml
```

Now, you can move this to a root directory called Base and create a separate directory called overlays at the same level as the Base directory. Inside overlays, you can have separate directories for each of the environments (dev, test, prod, etc.) along with their respective customized version of files.

```
Base/
    ├── deployment.yaml
    ├── service.yaml
    ├── config.properties
    └── kustomization.yaml
overlays/
    ├── dev/
    │   ├── kustomization.yaml
    │   ├── replicas.yaml
    │   └── config.properties
    └── stage/
            ├── kustomization.yaml
            ├── replicas.yaml
            └── config.properties
```

This structure allows you to maintain a single source of truth (base) while specifying environment-specific variations/customizations through overlays.

Let's assume you have a use case below:

- Development-specific deployments should be deployed inside the dev namespace.
- Stage-specific deployments should be deployed inside the stage namespace.
- For dev deployment, replicas should be two.
- For stage deployment, replicas should be four.

For the file `overlays/dev/kustomization.yaml`, you start by giving reference to the base folder under the base's top-level field and the fields that you wish to override, for example, namespace. You can also include custom fields such as replicas for each environment and create a separate replicas.yaml that has the configuration till the replicas field, and then you perform the same actions for the stage folder as well.

A sample `overlays/dev/kustomization.yaml` is shown below:

```
bases:
  - ../../base
namespace: dev
patches:
  - replicas.yaml
```

To apply these configurations, simply use

```
kubectl apply -k overlays/dev
```

Patches in Kustomize allow you to make delta modifications to your base configurations. This is particularly useful when you need to make environment-specific adjustments without duplicating entire configuration files.

CHAPTER 11   MANIFEST MANAGEMENT TOOLS

The following table shows a quick comparison between Helm and Kustomize.

	Kustomize	Helm
Native integration	Can be used from kubectl	No—installed separately
Ease of use	Beginner-friendly	Complex
Approach	Overlays	Template based
Mode	Declarative	Imperative
Bundling/packaging	No	Yes
Versioning/rollbacks	No	Yes

Summary

- Helm is a package manager for Kubernetes, similar to apt or yum, enabling simplified deployment and management of Kubernetes applications.

- Helm uses charts (bundles of YAML files, templates, and dependencies), repositories (central storage for charts), and releases (instances of running charts).

- Helm streamlines multi-environment deployment by allowing reusable charts with customizable values. yaml configurations, making application management efficient and scalable.

- Kustomize, in contrast, provides declarative configuration management without templating.

- It focuses on layering and organizing application configurations for multiple environments.

CHAPTER 11   MANIFEST MANAGEMENT TOOLS

- Using kustomization.yaml, Kustomize centralizes common settings (e.g., labels, annotations) and allows environment-specific overrides through overlays.

- This approach ensures a single source of truth with minimal duplication and enables configuration separation, such as managing configmaps and hierarchical structures for different environments.

- Both tools simplify Kubernetes application management but serve different use cases—Helm specializes in templating and reuse, while Kustomize focuses on declarative configuration and environment-specific adjustments.

CHAPTER 12

Authorization and Authentication

In this chapter, we will explore **authentication and authorization** in Kubernetes, two critical mechanisms that secure access to your cluster. You'll learn how Kubernetes verifies user identities through various authentication methods such as certificates, tokens, and external identity providers. We will then cover how **authorization** determines what authenticated users are allowed to do, focusing on mechanisms like **RBAC (role-based access control)**, **ABAC (attribute-based access control)**, **node**, and **webhooks**. By the end, you will understand how to implement fine-grained access control to protect your cluster and ensure only the right users and services can perform specific actions.

Authentication

In a client-server architecture such as Kubernetes, to be able to access or manage the server, the client should be able to authorize and authenticate.

Figure 12-1 shows the different types of authentication available.

CHAPTER 12   AUTHORIZATION AND AUTHENTICATION

Figure 12-1. Authentication types

Authentication is a way of validating the identity of a user (human user or service account) making a request to the API Server. Any user that presents a valid certificate signed by the cluster's certificate authority (CA) is considered authenticated. For service accounts, Kubernetes uses service account tokens that are automatically generated when the account is created. In simple terms, authentication is a way of validating the user's identity against who they say they are.

Authorization

Once the user is authenticated, the next step is to validate the level of access they have on the Kubernetes cluster and resources (i.e., what they are allowed to do and what they cannot do).

Figure 12-2 shows the available authorization types in Kubernetes.

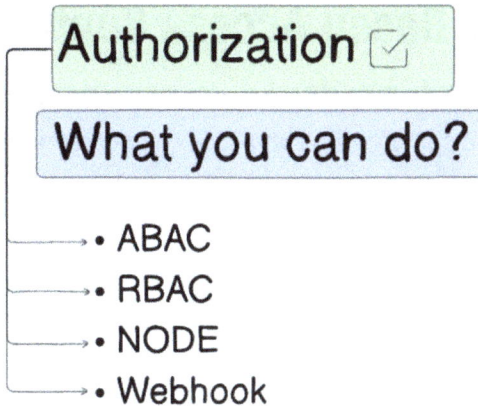

Figure 12-2. *Authorization types in Kubernetes*

Authorization Types

A Kubernetes API Server performs authorization based on the below modes:

- **AlwaysAllow**: All requests are allowed (a huge security risk).

- **AlwaysDeny**: All requests are denied by default.

- **ABAC**: Attribute-based access control.

- **RBAC**: Role-based access control.

- **Node**: Authorize Kubelet for certain actions on the node.

- **Webhook**: Event-based authorization through a webhook REST call.

CHAPTER 12   AUTHORIZATION AND AUTHENTICATION

RBAC (Role-Based Access Control)

RBAC in Kubernetes is a method for regulating access to the Kubernetes API. It allows you to specify who can access what resources within a Kubernetes cluster and what actions they can perform on those resources based on certain roles that they get assigned to. Instead of assigning permissions to individual users, it is easier to group related permissions together in a role and assign the role to a user or group.

Key concepts in Kubernetes RBAC:

> **Role**: Defines a set of permissions within a namespace. It contains rules that represent allowed operations on Kubernetes resources.
>
> **RoleBinding**: Grants the permissions defined in a Role to a user, group, or service account within a specific namespace.
>
> **ClusterRole**: Similar to a Role, but the ClusterRole is a cluster-scoped resource. It can be used to define permissions across all namespaces or for cluster-scoped resources.
>
> **ClusterRoleBinding**: Similar to RoleBinding, but it grants the permissions of a ClusterRole to a user, group, or service account across the entire cluster.

Figure 12-3 shows the hierarchy and relationship of role-based access control in Kubernetes.

CHAPTER 12 AUTHORIZATION AND AUTHENTICATION

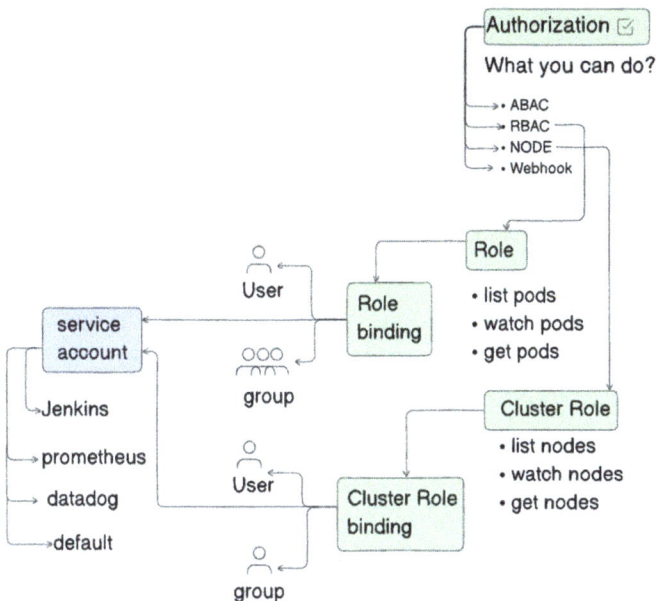

Figure 12-3. Role-based access control in Kubernetes

Authentication and Authorization in Kubernetes

To authenticate a new user in your Kubernetes cluster, we need to create the certificate issued by the cluster and then present that certificate to the Kubernetes API:

1) Create a private key using the command

   ```
   openssl genrsa -out piyush.key 2048
   ```

2) Generate a CSR (certificate signing request) file using the key generated in the previous step:

   ```
   openssl req -new -key piyush.key -out piyush.csr    -subj "/CN=piyush"
   ```

CHAPTER 12 AUTHORIZATION AND AUTHENTICATION

3) Create a CertificateSigningRequest.
   We need to obtain the value from piyush.csr generated in the previous step, encode it in base64, and then remove the trailing space, or you can use the below command:

   ```
   cat piyush.csr | base64 | tr -d "\"
   ```

   Once you have the value, you can create the below YAML and add the value in the request field (remember this is a base64-encoded value):

   ```
   cat <<EOF | kubectl apply -f -
   apiVersion: certificates.k8s.io/v1
   kind: CertificateSigningRequest
   metadata:
     name: myuser
   spec:
     request: <encoded string>
     signerName: kubernetes.io/kube-API Server-client
     expirationSeconds: 86400  # one day
     usages:
     - client auth
   EOF
   ```

4) If the above YAML is applied correctly, you can get the list of CSR using the command

   ```
   kubectl get csr
   ```

5) As an admin, you can approve the CSR using the below command:

   ```
   kubectl certificate approve myuser
   ```

Figure 12-4 shows the certification creation and approval process in Kubernetes.

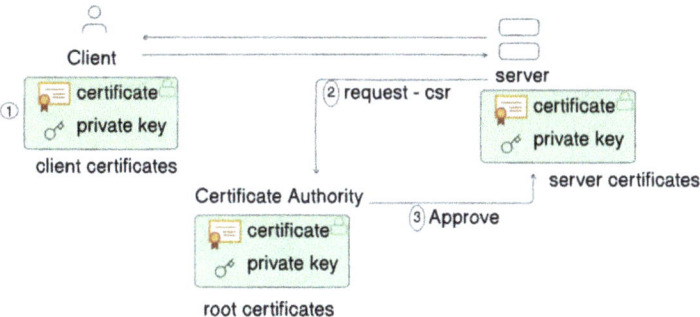

Figure 12-4. Certification signing request creation and approval process

6) Once the certificate is approved, you can retrieve the certificate from the CSR object:

kubectl get csr myuser -o yaml

The certificate value is in base64-encoded format under status.certificate; make sure to decode the value as it is base64 encoded:

<certificate> | base64 -d > piyush.crt

As your user has just been created, by default it should not have any access to the cluster, you can verify this by using the below command:

kubectl auth can-i get pods --as piyush
no

(This should return the output as no.)

CHAPTER 12   AUTHORIZATION AND AUTHENTICATION

7) Once the user is created, the next part of authorization is what the user can do in the cluster. We can do that via role and rolebinding. Let's assume the cluster is a pre-prod cluster and developers should only have read-only access, so we can create the role with only get and list access on the workloads as below:

```
kubectl create role developer --verb=get \ --verb=list --resource=pods
```

8) Now, we can attach the role to the user or the group using the rolebinding:

```
kubectl create rolebinding developer-binding --role=developer --user=piyush
```

9) After applying the rolebinding, the user piyush should have the access to get and list pods on the cluster:

```
kubectl auth can-i get pods --as piyush
yes
```

(This should return the output as yes.)

10) To log in as user piyush, you need to set the credentials in the Kubeconfig file and context:

```
kubectl config set-credentials piyush \ --client-key=piyush.key \ --client-certificate=piyush.crt \ --embed-certs=true
```

CHAPTER 12   AUTHORIZATION AND AUTHENTICATION

What Is Kubeconfig?

kubectl uses the Kubeconfig file to authenticate and authorize a user to the cluster that includes your client key and certificates. By default, it uses the kubeconfig file from $HOME/.kube/config; you can also point it to a separate file using the flag –kubeconfig=<path to config> or by setting the environment variable KUBECONFIG=<path to config>.

```
kubectl config set-context piyush \
  --cluster=kind-cka-cluster --user=piyush
kubectl config use-context piyush
```

You can validate whether you are logged in successfully and what access you have:

```
kubectl auth whoami
kubectl get pods  # this should return the running pods
kubectl get svc  # This should show the forbidden error
```

Why? Because we only granted the get/list pod access and not the service access.

Similarly, we can grant access to cluster-scoped resources such as nodes. To grant access to a cluster scope resource, we can use ClusterRole and ClusterRoleBinding instead of Role and RoleBinding:

```
kubectl create clusterrole node-reader --verb=get,list,watch --resource=node
kubectl create clusterrolebinding node-reader-binding  --clusterrole=node-reader --user=piyush
# Validate the access
kubectl auth can-i get nodes --as piyush
yes
```

(This should return the output as yes.)

117

To interact with the cluster, you can use the below command:

```
kubectl get pods --kubeconfig config
```

Normally, kubectl uses your local $HOME/.kube/config file for authentication, so you don't have to pass the --kubeconfig parameter in every command. You can use the below command:

```
kubectl get pods
```

The below command shows an API call using raw arguments:

```
kubectl get --raw /api/v1/namespaces/default/pods \
  --server https://localhost:64418 \
  --client-key piyush.key \
  --client-certificate piyush.crt \
  --certificate-authority ca.crt
```

> **Note** While using Kubeconfig, you don't have to specify the client-key, certificate, etc.; kubeconfig takes care of them.

Service Account

There are two types of accounts in Kubernetes that interact with the cluster. These could be user accounts used by humans, such as Kubernetes admins, developers, operators, etc., and service accounts primarily used by other applications/bots or Kubernetes components to interact with other services.

CHAPTER 12   AUTHORIZATION AND AUTHENTICATION

The below commands can be used to create and manage a service account:

```
kubectl create sa <saname>
kubectl get sa
kubectl describe sa <saname> -n <namespace_name>
```

Then you can add role and rolebinding to grant access. Kubernetes also creates one default service account in each of the default namespaces such as kube-system, kube-node-lease, and so on.

Summary

- Kubernetes uses authentication and authorization mechanisms to secure access to the cluster.

- **Authentication** verifies the identity of a user (human or service account) interacting with the cluster. Users authenticate through certificates signed by the cluster's certificate authority (CA), while service accounts use automatically generated tokens.

- **Authorization** defines what actions authenticated users can perform on the cluster.

Kubernetes supports various authorization modes:

- **AlwaysAllow/AlwaysDeny**: Permits or blocks all requests (not recommended)

- **ABAC**: Attribute-based access control

- **RBAC**: Role-based access control

- **Node**: Access that Kubelet gets to perform certain actions on a node

- **Webhook**: Webhook-based authorization

CHAPTER 12   AUTHORIZATION AND AUTHENTICATION

Role-based access control (RBAC) manages access through roles and bindings:

- **Role/RoleBinding**: Namespace-specific permissions and bindings.

- **ClusterRole/ClusterRoleBinding**: Cluster-wide access and bindings.

- Access is managed via kubeconfig files containing credentials and certificates, which ensure secure interactions with the Kubernetes API.

CHAPTER 13

Network Policies

Network policy allows you to control the inbound and outbound traffic to and from the cluster. For example, you can specify a deny-all network policy that restricts all incoming traffic to the cluster, or you can create an allow network policy that will only allow certain services to be accessed by certain pods on a specific port.

If you are using the KinD cluster, you need to add the networking setting inside the kind manifest to disable the default CNI and advertise the pod Classless Inter-Domain Routing (CIDR) as below (yes, we will discuss CNI after this):

```
kind: Cluster
apiVersion: kind.x-k8s.io/v1alpha4
nodes:
- role: control-plane
  extraPortMappings:
  - containerPort: 30001
    hostPort: 30001
- role: worker
- role: worker
networking:
  disableDefaultCNI: true
  podSubnet: 192.168.0.0/16
```

CNI (Container Network Interface)

CNI stands for Container Network Interface. It's a standard for configuring network interfaces in Linux containers, used by container orchestrators like Kubernetes. CNI provides a framework for plugins to manage container networking, allowing different networking solutions to be easily integrated. To implement a network policy in a Kubernetes cluster, you need to have CNI plugins installed, as it does not come with a vanilla Kubernetes installation.

Below are some popular CNI plugins:

1. Weave-net
2. Flannel and Kindnet (**doesn't support network policies**)
3. Calico
4. Cilium

CNI is deployed as a DaemonSet; hence, CNI pods will be running on each node in the cluster.

CNI Installation

To install a CNI plugin such as Calico, you can follow the below documentation:

https://docs.tigera.io/calico/latest/getting-started/kubernetes/kind

CHAPTER 13   NETWORK POLICIES

Network Policy Implementation

For instance, we have to restrict the access within a Kubernetes cluster in which only backend pods should be allowed to access the database pods, and other pods, such as frontend ones, should not have access to the backend pods.

Figure 13-1 shows a sample network policy that allows only the backend pod to access the my-sql pod and restricts access from the frontend pod to the my-sql pod.

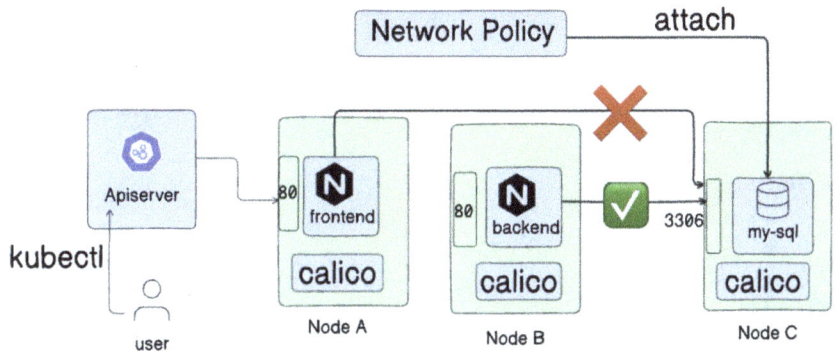

Figure 13-1. *Network policy sample that only allows the backend pod to access the my-sql pod*

We start with creating three Kubernetes pods, such as frontend, backend, and database, and expose them through the services. You can use the below sample YAML for the same:

```
apiVersion: v1
kind: Pod
metadata:
  name: frontend
  labels:
    role: frontend
```

123

CHAPTER 13   NETWORK POLICIES

```
spec:
  containers:
  - name: nginx
    image: nginx
    ports:
    - name: http
      containerPort: 80
      protocol: TCP
---
apiVersion: v1
kind: Service
metadata:
  name: frontend
  labels:
    role: frontend
spec:
  selector:
    role: frontend
  ports:
  - protocol: TCP
    port: 80
    targetPort: 80
---
apiVersion: v1
kind: Pod
metadata:
  name: backend
  labels:
    role: backend
spec:
  containers:
```

```
    - name: nginx
      image: nginx
      ports:
      - name: http
        containerPort: 80
        protocol: TCP
---
apiVersion: v1
kind: Service
metadata:
  name: backend
  labels:
    role: backend
spec:
  selector:
    role: backend
  ports:
  - protocol: TCP
    port: 80
    targetPort: 80
---
apiVersion: v1
kind: Service
metadata:
  name: db
  labels:
    name: mysql
spec:
  selector:
    name: mysql
```

CHAPTER 13 NETWORK POLICIES

```
  ports:
  - protocol: TCP
    port: 3306
    targetPort: 3306
---
apiVersion: v1
kind: Pod
metadata:
  name: mysql
  labels:
    name: mysql
spec:
  containers:
    - name: mysql
      image: mysql:latest
      env:
        - name: "MYSQL_USER"
          value: "mysql"
        - name: "MYSQL_PASSWORD"
          value: "mysql"
        - name: "MYSQL_DATABASE"
          value: "testdb"
        - name: "MYSQL_ROOT_PASSWORD"
          value: "verysecure"
      ports:
        - name: http
          containerPort: 3306
          protocol: TCP
```

Now the next part is to create a network policy that will only allow the MySQL pod to be accessed by the backend pod and attach the policy to the MySQL pod through labels and selectors:

```
apiVersion: networking.k8s.io/v1
kind: NetworkPolicy
metadata:
  name: db-test
spec:
  podSelector:
    matchLabels:
      name: mysql
  policyTypes:
  - Ingress
  ingress:
  - from:
    - podSelector:
        matchLabels:
          role: backend
    ports:
    - port: 3306
```

If you noticed the network policy YAML, we have a few additional fields:

> **PolicyTypes: Ingress**: Valid values are Ingress and Egress to control inbound and outbound access, respectively. With Ingress, we have provided an additional rule that matches the label with the pod label. In this example, we are allowing the pod with the label role:backend to have inbound access to the pod on which this network policy is attached.
>
> **PodSelector**: This field is responsible for attaching the network policy to the pod with the matching label name: mysql.

To test the changes, perform the below steps:

- Log in to the frontend pod using kubectl exec and try doing a curl on the MySQL service; this curl should throw an error.

- Log in to the backend pod using kubectl exec and try doing a curl on the MySQL service; this curl should show a successful response.

If you are facing issues, check the above steps along with the Calico health status.

Summary

- Network policies in Kubernetes control inbound and outbound traffic to and from the cluster. They allow you to define rules, such as restricting all incoming traffic or permitting access to specific services on designated ports.

- Network policies require a Container Network Interface (CNI) plugin for implementation, as Kubernetes does not provide this functionality by default.

- CNI is a standard for configuring network interfaces in containers, enabling seamless integration of various networking solutions.

- Popular CNI plugins include Calico, Weave Net, and Cilium, with some (e.g., Flannel, Kindnet) not supporting network policies.

- CNI is deployed as a DaemonSet, ensuring networking functionality across all cluster nodes.

CHAPTER 13   NETWORK POLICIES

- A common use case is restricting access between pods, such as allowing only backend pods to access database pods while blocking other pods (e.g., frontend pods).

- Network policies use labels and selectors to enforce these rules.

Workloads and Scheduling Review Questions

- Create a deployment that initially has two replicas and uses nginx as a container image, then scale the deployment to four replicas using the kubectl command.

- Expose the deployment as a nodePort service on port 8080.

- Check for the pods that have label env:demo and redirect the pod names to a file pod.txt.

- Create an nginx pod; ensure it is running. Edit the pod and add an init container that uses a busybox image and run the command sleep 10;echo "hello world".

- Create a pod and force schedule it on worker node 01.

- Create a multi-container pod with the images as redis and memcached.

PART III

Storage

This topic covers 10% of the exam and focuses on the following:

- Implementing StorageClasses and dynamic volume provisioning
- Configuring volume types, access modes, and reclaim policies
- Managing PersistentVolumes and PersistentVolumeClaims

CHAPTER 14

Kubernetes Installation Using Kubeadm

In one of the previous chapters, we did the Kubernetes installation on KinD as it is lightweight and easy to set up. While KinD is an ideal choice for local development and for learning purposes, it does not provide the capabilities of a full-fledged production-grade Kubernetes cluster. In this chapter, we will perform the Kubernetes installation using the Kubeadm tool.

Prerequisites for Installation

Kubeadm is a tool to bootstrap the Kubernetes cluster, which installs all the control plane components (API Server, ETCD, controller manager, and scheduler) as static pods and gets the cluster ready for you. You can perform various tasks such as node initialization, node reset, joining worker nodes with control plane nodes, etc.

Till now, we were using a KinD cluster, but now we will create a fresh multi-node cluster on cloud virtual machines using Kubeadm.

High-level steps of the installation will be as follows.

Figure 14-1 shows a high-level flow of Kubernetes installation steps using Kubeadm.

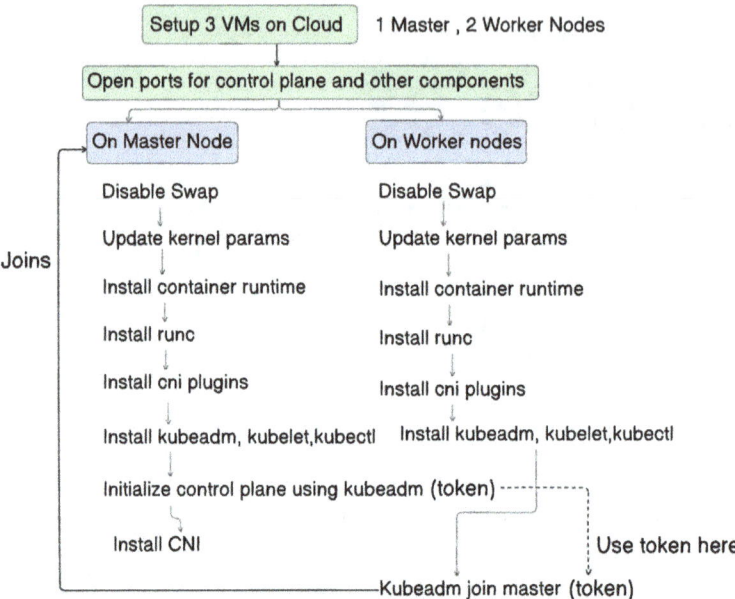

Figure 14-1. *Kubernetes installation steps using Kubeadm*

Virtual Machine Setup

For this step, you can use a virtualization software (VirtualBox, Multipass, etc.) that is able to create three virtual machines, or you can use virtual machines using any cloud provider.

In this book, I will be using Amazon EC2 servers for this purpose. You can go to the AWS console and provision three EC2 servers, one for master nodes and two for worker nodes.

CHAPTER 14 KUBERNETES INSTALLATION USING KUBEADM

Open the Required Ports for Networking

Security groups in AWS restrict access on certain ports to and from certain sources and destinations. In Kubernetes, different components will be communicating with each other on certain ports; hence, we need to allow the access as below.

Figure 14-2 shows all the ports that we need to open between different Kubernetes components for communication.

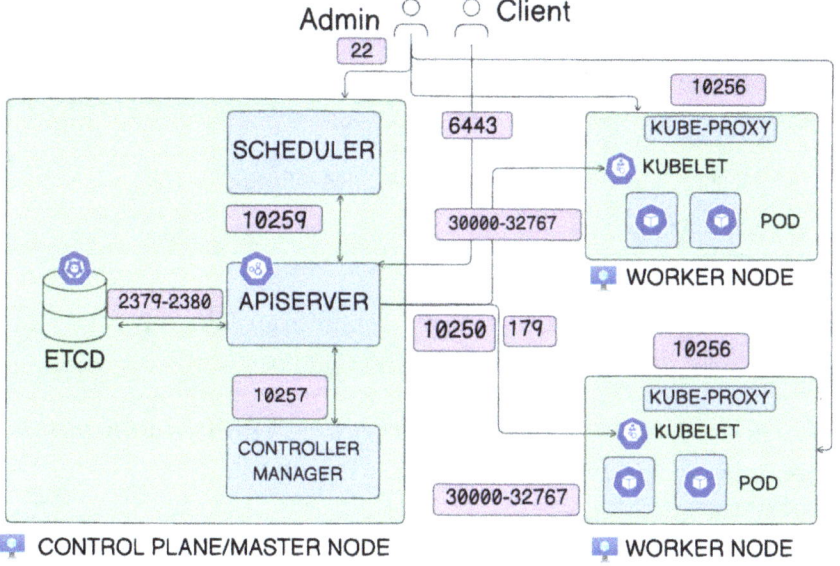

Figure 14-2. *Ports required for communication between Kubernetes components*

Configure Security Groups

Create the security group using the details from Table 14-1 for the control plane node and attach it to the EC2 server that acts as a master node.

135

CHAPTER 14 KUBERNETES INSTALLATION USING KUBEADM

Table 14-1. *The ports needed in master node for inbound/outbound connectivity within the cluster*

Protocol	Direction	Port Range	Purpose	Used By
TCP	Inbound	6443	Kubernetes API Server	All
TCP	Inbound	2379–2380	ETCD server client API	kube-API Server, ETCD
TCP	Inbound	10250	Kubelet API	Self, control plane
TCP	Inbound	10259	kube-scheduler	Self
TCP	Inbound	10257	kube-controller-manager	Self
TCP	Inbound/outbound	179	Calico networking	All

Create the security group using the details from Table 14-2 and attach it to both the EC2 servers that act as worker nodes.

Table 14-2. *The ports needed in worker nodes for inbound/outbound connectivity within the cluster*

Protocol	Direction	Port Range	Purpose	Used By
TCP	Inbound	10250	Kubelet API	Self, control plane
TCP	Inbound	10256	kube-proxy	Self, load balancers
TCP	Inbound	30000–32767	NodePort services	All
TCP	Inbound/outbound	179	Calico networking	All

> **Note** Disable source/destination checks for master and worker nodes from the EC2 console.

Set Up Master Node to Deploy Kubernetes Components

SSH into the master node and perform the below steps:

1) Disable swap:

    ```
    swapoff -a
    sudo sed -i '/ swap / s/^\(.*\)$/#\1/g' \
    /etc/fstab
    ```

2) Forward IPv4 and let iptables see bridged traffic:

    ```
    cat <<EOF | sudo tee /etc/modules-load.d/k8s.conf
    overlay
    br_netfilter
    EOF

    sudo modprobe overlay
    sudo modprobe br_netfilter

    # sysctl params required by setup, params persist across reboots
    cat <<EOF | sudo tee /etc/sysctl.d/k8s.conf
    net.bridge.bridge-nf-call-iptables  = 1
    net.bridge.bridge-nf-call-ip6tables = 1
    net.ipv4.ip_forward                 = 1
    EOF
    ```

```
# Apply sysctl params without reboot
sudo sysctl --system

# Verify that the br_netfilter, overlay modules are
loaded by running the following commands:
lsmod | grep br_netfilter
lsmod | grep overlay

# Verify that the net.bridge.bridge-nf-call-iptables,
net.bridge.bridge-nf-call-ip6tables, and net.ipv4.
ip_forward system variables are set to 1 in your sysctl
config by running the following command:
sysctl net.bridge.bridge-nf-call-iptables net.bridge.
bridge-nf-call-ip6tables net.ipv4.ip_forward
```

3) Install a container runtime (use the latest version):

```
curl -LO https://github.com/containerd/containerd/
releases/download/v1.7.14/containerd-1.7.14-linux-
amd64.tar.gz
sudo tar Cxzvf /usr/local containerd-1.7.14-linux-
amd64.tar.gz
curl -LO https://raw.githubusercontent.com/containerd/
containerd/main/containerd.service
sudo mkdir -p /usr/local/lib/systemd/system/
sudo mv containerd.service /usr/local/lib/
systemd/system/
sudo mkdir -p /etc/containerd
containerd config default | sudo tee /etc/containerd/
config.toml
sudo sed -i 's/SystemdCgroup \= false/SystemdCgroup
\= true/g' /etc/containerd/config.toml
```

CHAPTER 14 KUBERNETES INSTALLATION USING KUBEADM

```
sudo systemctl daemon-reload
sudo systemctl enable --now containerd

# Check that containerd service is up and running
systemctl status containerd
```

4) Install Runc (latest version):

```
curl -LO https://github.com/opencontainers/runc/
releases/download/v1.1.12/runc.amd64

sudo install -m 755 runc.amd64 \ /usr/local/sbin/runc
```

5) Install the CNI plugin such as Calico:

```
curl -LO https://github.com/containernetworking/
plugins/releases/download/v1.5.0/cni-plugins-linux-
amd64-v1.5.0.tgz

sudo mkdir -p /opt/cni/bin

sudo tar Cxzvf /opt/cni/bin \
cni-plugins-linux-amd64-v1.5.0.tgz
```

6) Install Kubeadm, Kubelet and Kubectl

```
sudo apt-get update
sudo apt-get install -y apt-transport-https
ca-certificates curl gpg

curl -fsSL https://pkgs.k8s.io/core:/stable:/
v1.29/deb/Release.key | sudo gpg --dearmor -o
/etc/apt/keyrings/kubernetes-apt-keyring.gpg
echo 'deb [signed-by=/etc/apt/keyrings/kubernetes-
apt-keyring.gpg] https://pkgs.k8s.io/core:/stable:/
v1.29/deb/ /' | sudo tee /etc/apt/sources.list.d/
kubernetes.list
```

CHAPTER 14   KUBERNETES INSTALLATION USING KUBEADM

```
sudo apt-get update
sudo apt-get install -y kubelet=1.29.6-1.1
kubeadm=1.29.6-1.1 kubectl=1.29.6-1.1 --allow-
downgrades --allow-change-held-packages
sudo apt-mark hold kubelet kubeadm kubectl

kubeadm version
kubelet --version
kubectl version --client
```

7) Configure crictl to work with containerD:

```
sudo crictl config runtime-endpoint
unix:///var/run/containerd/containerd.sock
```

8) Initialize the control plane:

```
sudo kubeadm init \
--pod-network-cidr=192.168.0.0/16 \
--API Server-advertise-address=<> \
--node-name master
```

Note APIServer-advertise-address is the private IP of the master node.

---

9) Prepare kubeconfig:

```
mkdir -p $HOME/.kube
sudo cp -i /etc/kubernetes/admin.conf
$HOME/.kube/config
sudo chown $(id -u):$(id -g)
$HOME/.kube/config
```

CHAPTER 14   KUBERNETES INSTALLATION USING KUBEADM

10) Install Calico:

    ```
    kubectl create -f
                    https://raw.githubusercontent.com/
                    projectcalico/
    calico/v3.28.0/manifests/tigera-operator.yaml
    ```

    ```
    curl https://raw.githubusercontent.com/projectcalico/
    calico/v3.28.0/manifests/custom-resources.yaml -O
    ```

    ```
    kubectl apply -f custom-resources.yaml
    ```

11) SSH into the worker nodes and perform steps (1–7) on both nodes.

12) Run the command generated in step 8 on the master node, which is similar to below:

    ```
    sudo kubeadm join API Server:6443 \
    --token xxxxx \ --discovery-token-ca-cert-hash
    sha256:xxx
    ```

13) If you forgot to copy the command, you can execute the below command on the master node to generate the join command again.

    ```
    kubeadm token create --print-join-command
    ```

Validating the Installation

If all the above steps were completed, you should be able to run `kubectl get nodes` on the master node, and it should return all the three nodes in ready status.

Also, make sure all the pods are up and running by using the command as follows: `kubectl get pods -A`.

CHAPTER 14   KUBERNETES INSTALLATION USING KUBEADM

Implement and Configure a Highly Available Control Plane

If you are running a self-hosted production Kubernetes cluster, you should be setting up the high availability for control plane nodes as well. This part is not required if you are using a managed Kubernetes service such as Azure Kubernetes Service (AKS), Elastic Kubernetes Service (EKS), or Google Kubernetes Engine (GKE); however, you need to take care of these steps in the case of a self-hosted cluster.

You can use either of the two approaches to set up a highly available control plane using Kubeadm:

- **With Stacked Control Plane Nodes:** You create multiple control plane nodes with an API Server and ETCD.

- **With an External ETCD Cluster:** You create separate nodes for the API Server and separate nodes for ETCD members; this approach will need more infrastructure; hence, more cost associated with it.

Note   In this chapter, we will focus on stacked control plane nodes.

High Availability Using Stacked Control Plane Prerequisites

- At least three machines for control plane nodes that meet Kubeadm's minimum requirements, such as a supported OS, 2GB RAM, two CPUs, etc. An odd number of machines helps with leader selection in the case of host or zone failure.

CHAPTER 14 KUBERNETES INSTALLATION USING KUBEADM

- At least three machines for worker nodes that meet Kubeadm's minimum requirements, such as a supported OS, 2GB RAM, two CPUs, etc.
- All required ports are open between nodes.
- Kubeadm, kubelet, and kubectl installed on all nodes.
- Container runtime installed and configured.
- All machines have access to each other on a network.
- Superuser privileges on all machines (sudo or root access).

Load Balancer Configuration

The first critical component in your HA setup is a properly configured TCP forwarding load balancer for the API Server. This load balancer will act as the front door for all incoming requests and redirect the traffic to the API Servers as the backend on port 6443.

We need to ensure the load balancer can communicate with all control plane nodes on the API Server port and its address matches Kubeadm's ControlPlaneEndpoint.

Figure 14-3 shows the Kubernetes sample architecture diagram with a stacked control plane that uses a load balancer.

CHAPTER 14 KUBERNETES INSTALLATION USING KUBEADM

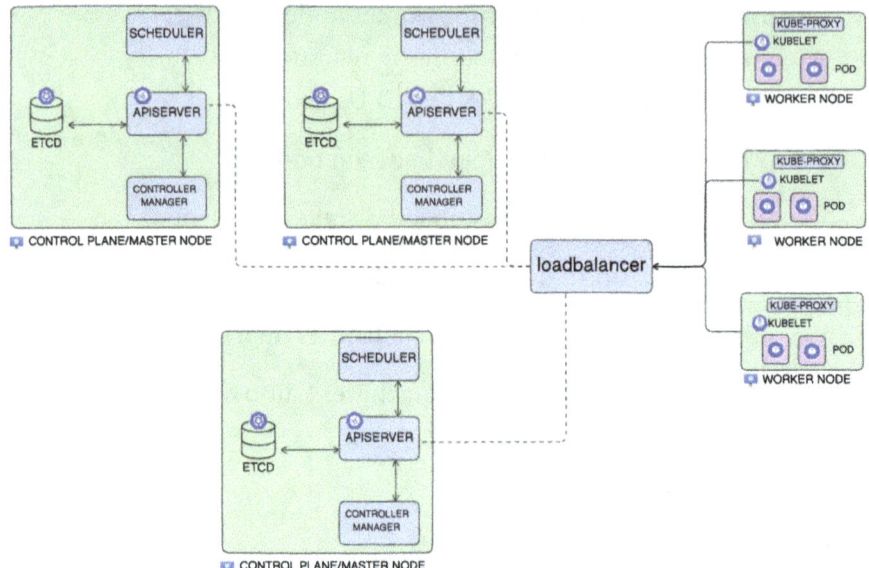

Figure 14-3. *Sample Kubernetes stacked control plane architecture for high availability*

Add the first control plane node to the load balancer and test the connection:

```
nc -v <LOAD_BALANCER_IP> <PORT>
```

Note Initially, you'll receive a "connection refused" error since the API Server isn't running. A timeout indicates a load balancer configuration issue that needs immediate attention.

Add the remaining control plane nodes to the load balancer's target group.

Initializing the First Control Plane Node

The first control plane node serves as the bootstrap node for your cluster. Here's how to initialize it:

```
sudo kubeadm init --control-plane-endpoint \ <LOAD_BALANCER_DNS:LOAD_BALANCER_PORT> \
--upload-certs
```

> --**control-plane-endpoint**: Specifies your load balancer's DNS and port.
>
> --**upload-certs**: Enables automatic certificate distribution across control plane nodes.
>
> **Optional**: Use --**pod-network-cidr** if your CNI plugin requires it.

The output looks similar to

```
...
You can now join any number of control-plane node by running
the following command on each as a root:
    kubeadm join 192.168.0.200:6443 --token <token>
    --discovery-token-ca-cert-hash sha256:<cert_hash>
    --control-plane --certificate-key <cert-key>

Please note that the certificate-key gives access to cluster
sensitive data, keep it secret!
As a safeguard, uploaded-certs will be deleted in two hours;
If necessary, you can use kubeadm init phase upload-certs to
reload certs afterward.

Then you can join any number of worker nodes by running the
following on each as root:
    kubeadm join 192.168.0.200:6443 --token <token>
    --discovery-token-ca-cert-hash sha256:<cert_hash>
...
```

Certificate Management

Certificates are crucial for cluster security. When using --upload-certs, certificates are encrypted and stored in the **kubeadm-certs** secret. The decryption key and kubeadm-certs secret expire after two hours by default.

To regenerate certificates, run this command:

```
sudo kubeadm init phase upload-certs --upload-certs
```

You can also generate a custom certificate key during init and use it later during join:

```
kubeadm certs certificate-key
```

Install the CNI Plugin

You can now install the CNI plugin, such as Calico/Cilium, etc., as per your requirements. If you want to install Calico, the steps used in the previous chapter can be followed here.

Verify the Pods

```
kubectl get pod -n kube-system
```

Steps for Each of the Control Plane Nodes

Log in to each of the additional control plane nodes and join them to the master control plane node using the command generated earlier that looks something like

```
kubeadm join 192.168.0.200:6443 --token <token> --discovery-token-ca-cert-hash sha256:<cert_hash>
```

Note You can also run the join command parallelly from multiple nodes.

Steps for Worker Nodes

Join the worker nodes to the control plane using the same command:

```
kubeadm join 192.168.0.200:6443 --token <token> --discovery-token-ca-cert-hash sha256:<cert_hash>
```

Summary

- In this chapter, we discussed the process of setting up a Kubernetes cluster using Kubeadm.

- Kubeadm is a powerful tool for bootstrapping Kubernetes clusters by installing control plane components like API Server, ETCD, Controller Manager, and Scheduler as static pods.

- Kubeadm also facilitates tasks such as node initialization, resetting nodes, and joining worker nodes to the control plane.

- The installation process includes provisioning three virtual machines (one master and two worker nodes) using cloud providers like AWS or virtualization software.

- Security groups must be configured to enable component communication, and source/destination checks should be disabled.

- Key setup steps include disabling swap, configuring networking, and installing necessary components such as the container runtime, CNI plugins, Kubeadm, Kubelet, and Kubectl.

- After initializing the control plane and setting up the kubeconfig, a pod network like Calico is deployed for networking as a DaemonSet.

- Worker nodes are prepared with similar configurations and joined to the cluster using a token.

- Once all steps are completed, the cluster can be validated to ensure all nodes and pods are running correctly.

CHAPTER 15

Storage in Kubernetes

Storage in Kubernetes is handled by something known as PersistentVolume and PersistentVolumeClaim. In simple words, a storage admin creates the volume, which is the representation of a physical storage that can be consumed by other users and applications; this volume is called a PersistentVolume.

The PersistentVolume has a storage capacity, access mode, StorageClass, etc., using which a user or an application can request a slice of this volume by creating an object called a PersistentVolumeClaim.

Figure 15-1 shows a high-level relationship between PersistentVolumes and PersistentVolumeClaims.

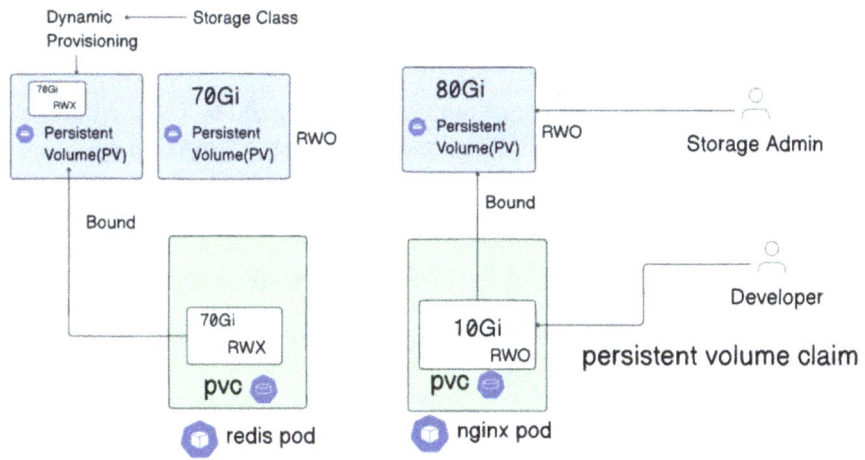

Figure 15-1. *PersistentVolumes and PersistentVolumeClaims in Kubernetes*

To successfully bind a PersistentVolumeClaim (PVC) with the PersistentVolume (PV), you need to make sure that their properties, such as access mode and StorageClass, match with each other, and the request capacity should be less than or equal to the available capacity.

Lifecycle of a Volume and Claim

There are two ways PVs can be provisioned in a Kubernetes cluster:

- Static provisioning
- Dynamic provisioning

Static Provisioning

A cluster/storage administrator creates the PersistentVolume(s), which are available to be consumed by users and applications and exist in the Kubernetes API.

Dynamic Provisioning

When the available PVC does not match the requested PVCs, the cluster may dynamically provision a volume for that matching PVC. This provisioning can be done through a StorageClass that should already exist in the cluster.

StorageClass is helpful to provision the PV based on the certain storage and performance requirements.

PersistentVolume

A PersistentVolume (PV) is a piece of storage in the cluster that has been provisioned by an administrator or dynamically provisioned using a StorageClass.

Key features include

> **Lifecycle**: PVs exist independently of the pods that use them and can be reused or reclaimed as per the defined policies.
>
> **Attributes**: Includes information about the storage capacity, access modes, and the StorageClass it belongs to.
>
> **Reclaim Policy**: Defines what happens to the volume when it is released by a PVC (e.g., retain, delete, or recycle).

PersistentVolumeClaim

PersistentVolumeClaim (PVC) is a request for storage by a user or application. It is used to request a specific amount of storage with certain attributes (like access modes) from available PersistentVolumes.

Key features include

> **Request**: Allows users to specify the amount of storage required and the access mode, for example, 10GB.
>
> **Binding**: PVCs are bound to available PVs that match the requested criteria. If a suitable PV is found, it will be bound to the PVC.
>
> **Dynamic Provisioning**: If no suitable PV is available, the PVC may trigger the creation of a new PV based on the StorageClass.

In Kubernetes, access modes and reclaim policies are key attributes for managing PersistentVolumes (PVs) and PersistentVolumeClaims (PVCs). They define how storage resources are accessed and managed within the cluster.

Access Modes

Access modes define how a PersistentVolume (PV) can be mounted and accessed by containers. They specify the level of access a pod has to the volume. Kubernetes supports the following access modes:

- **ReadWriteOnce (RWO):** This is useful for applications that need to write data and can operate from a single node, such as a single-instance database or an application server.

- **ReadOnlyMany (ROX):** Suitable for scenarios where multiple nodes need to read data from the volume but not write to it, such as serving static content or configuration files.

- **ReadWriteMany (RWX):** This mode is used for applications that require concurrent read and write access from multiple nodes, such as distributed file systems or shared data storage solutions.

Reclaim Policies

Reclaim policies determine what happens to a PersistentVolume (PV) when its associated PersistentVolumeClaim (PVC) is deleted. They define the lifecycle of the PV and how it should be handled after it is no longer needed:

> **Retain:** The PV is retained and not deleted after the PVC is deleted. The volume will remain in the cluster and must be manually reclaimed by an administrator.

Delete: The PV and its associated storage are deleted when the PVC is deleted. This is often used with dynamically provisioned volumes where the underlying storage is managed by the cloud provider or storage system.

Recycle (Deprecated): The PV is scrubbed and made available for reuse when the PVC is deleted. Scrubbing typically involves deleting the data on the volume before it is made available for new claims.

Demo Provisioning a Pod with Persistent Storage

We will perform a small demo of provisioning persistent storage and how a pod consumes the storage:

1) Provision a PersistentVolume that has the capacity of 1Gi, access mode as `ReadWriteOnce`, and `hostpath` in your local Kubernetes node.

   ```
   apiVersion: v1
   kind: PersistentVolume
   metadata:
     name: task-pv-volume
     labels:
       type: local
   spec:
     capacity:
       storage: 1Gi
     accessModes:
       - ReadWriteOnce
     hostPath:
       path: "/home/ubuntu/storage-demo"
   ```

2) Create a PVC that request the slice of the above PV.

```
apiVersion: v1
kind: PersistentVolumeClaim
metadata:
 name: task-pv-claim
spec:
  accessModes:
  - ReadWriteOnce
  resources:
   requests:
    storage: 500Mi
```

Note If you run a kubectl describe on the PVC, it should show the status as bound; if that is not the case, you need to check accessModes, storage, etc., or check the events printed by the command.

3) Create the pod to consume the volume.

Now you can create a sample pod with additional fields such as volumes inside the spec, which should have the reference of PersistentVolumeClaim and volume mounts inside the container, which should point to the location inside the container.

```
apiVersion: v1
kind: Pod
metadata:
  name: task-pv-pod
spec:
```

```
    volumes:
      - name: task-pv-storage
        persistentVolumeClaim:
          claimName: task-pv-claim
    containers:
      - name: task-pv-container
        image: nginx
        ports:
          - containerPort: 80
            name: "http-server"
        volumeMounts:
          - mountPath: "/usr/share/nginx/html"
            name: task-pv-storage
```

StorageClass

StorageClass provides a way to describe the "classes" of storage offered by cluster administrators. Different classes may offer different quality-of-service levels, backup policies, or arbitrary policies determined by cluster administrators.

StorageClass enables dynamic volume provisioning, allowing storage volumes to be created on demand. Without StorageClass, cluster administrators would need to manually provision PersistentVolumes.

The following YAML snippet explains how to use a StorageClass:

```
apiVersion: storage.k8s.io/v1
kind: StorageClass
metadata:
  name: standard
provisioner: ebs.csi.aws.com
reclaimPolicy: Retain # default value is Delete
allowVolumeExpansion: true
```

```
parameters:
  type: pd-standard
  encrypted: "true"
volumeBindingMode: WaitForFirstConsumer
allowedTopologies:
- matchLabelExpressions:
  - key: topology.kubernetes.io/zone
    values:
    - us-central-1a
    - us-central-1b
```

You might have noticed many additional fields that we have not discussed yet; let's understand these.

`provisioner: ebs.csi.aws.com` indicates this StorageClass uses the AWS EBS CSI driver for provisioning storage volumes. This provisioner creates AWS EBS volumes when PVCs request this StorageClass.

`Reclaim Policy` determines what happens to a PersistentVolume (PV) when its associated PersistentVolumeClaim (PVC) is deleted; we have already discussed reclaim policy in this chapter.

`allowVolumeExpansion:true` enables the ability to expand volumes after creation and allows users to increase PVC size without recreating the volume.

`parameters` describe volumes belonging to the StorageClass. Different provisioners support different parameters that can be used with the StorageClass, if you don't specify the parameter, some default values will be used based on the provisioner.

`volumeBindingMode` defines when the volume binding and dynamic provisioning should happen. Supported values are `Immediate` (default value) and `WaitForFirstConsumer`. Immediate mode guarantees immediate volume binding as soon as it is provisioned; however, `WaitForFirstConsumer` delays volume binding until a pod using the PVC is created.

`Topology Constraints` restricts volume provisioning to specific zones.

Default StorageClass

When you provision a Kubernetes cluster, you might get a pre-installed StorageClass that is marked as the default StorageClass. When you create a PVC without mentioning any StorageClass, it will use the default StorageClass to provision the storage for you. The default StorageClass might not be suitable for your workloads, or it could be too expensive for every use case, or it wouldn't provide you the performance that you need based on the workloads, and so on. In those cases, you might create a new StorageClass and change it to default. You can have multiple StorageClasses created, but only a single StorageClass can be used as a default StorageClass. Follow these steps to change the default StorageClass:

1. List all the StorageClasses in your cluster:

    ```
    kubectl get sc
    ```

    or

    ```
    kubectl get storageclass
    ```

    The output will be similar to this:

    ```
    NAME                 PROVISIONER              AGE
    standard (default)   kubernetes.io/gce-pd     1d
    custom               kubernetes.io/gce-pd     1d
    ```

> **Note** The default StorageClass should be marked as (default).

Patch the Annotation

The default StorageClass has an annotation storageclass.kubernetes.io/is-default-class set to true; to make the storageclass as non-default, we need to set the annotation to false using the below command:

CHAPTER 15   STORAGE IN KUBERNETES

```
kubectl patch storageclass standard -p '{"metadata":
{"annotations":{"storageclass.kubernetes.io/is-default-
class":"false"}}}'
```

Set the Annotation on a Different StorageClass

Using the similar command, you can mark your custom StorageClass as default:

```
kubectl patch storageclass custom -p '{"metadata":
{"annotations":{"storageclass.kubernetes.io/is-default-
class":"true"}}}'
```

Verify the Changes

```
kubectl get storageclass
NAME                PROVISIONER                AGE
standard            kubernetes.io/gce-pd       1d
custom (default)    kubernetes.io/gce-pd       1d
```

Once the StorageClass is created, you can use it by giving its reference inside the pod's specification as below:

```
apiVersion: v1
kind: PersistentVolumeClaim
metadata:
  name: task-pv-claim
spec:
  storageClassName: custom
  accessModes:
    - ReadWriteOnce
  resources:
    requests:
      storage: 500Mi
```

Summary

- Kubernetes handles storage through PersistentVolumes (PVs) and PersistentVolumeClaims (PVCs).

- **PersistentVolume (PV)**: Represents physical storage provisioned by an admin or dynamically created using a StorageClass. It includes attributes like storage capacity, access modes, and reclaim policies (e.g., retain, delete, or recycle).

- PVs exist independently of pods and can be reused or reclaimed as per policies.

- **PersistentVolumeClaim (PVC)**: A request for storage by users or applications. PVCs specify required attributes like capacity and access modes. They bind to suitable PVs or trigger dynamic provisioning through StorageClass when no matching PV is available.

- **Static Provisioning**: Admins pre-create PVs for use.

- **Dynamic Provisioning**: Kubernetes creates PVs on demand using a predefined StorageClass based on the requirements.

- StorageClass provides a way to describe the classes of storage offered by cluster administrators. If the storageClass field is omitted from the PVC manifest, the default StorageClass will be used to provision the volume.

- You can change the default StorageClass by patching the annotation on the StorageClass object.

CHAPTER 15   STORAGE IN KUBERNETES

Storage Review Questions

- Create a PersistentVolumeClaim (PVC) named mysql in the mysql namespace with the following specifications:
    - Access mode: ReadWrite Once
    - Storage: 250Mi
    - You must use the existing, retained PersistentVolume (PV)
    - Update the deployment to use the PVC you created in the previous step
- Create a PV with 1Gi capacity and mode readWriteOnce and no StorageClass; create a PVC with 500Mi storage and mode as readWriteOnce; it should be bounded with the PV. Create a pod that utilizes this PVC and use a mount path /data.
- Create a PVC with 10Mi, mount this PVC to the pod at /var/new-vol. Now, edit the PVC and increase the size from 10Mi to 50Mi.
- Create a sample StorageClass and update it to become the default storage class.

PART IV

Services and Networking

These topics cover 20% of the exam and focus on the following:

- Understanding host networking configuration on cluster nodes
- Understanding connectivity between pods
- Understanding ClusterIP, NodePort, and Load Balancer service types and endpoints
- Knowing how to use Ingress controllers and Ingress resources
- Knowing how to configure and use CoreDNS
- Choosing an appropriate Container Network Interface plugin
- Defining and enforcing network policies
- Using the Gateway API to manage Ingress traffic

CHAPTER 16

Kubernetes Networking

This chapter provides a foundational understanding of **Kubernetes networking**, a critical aspect of how pods communicate within a cluster and with the outside world.

Host Networking

In Kubernetes, networking is implemented at various levels and is one of the most crucial parts of the Kubernetes ecosystem. There could be communication happening at several layers, such as

- **Container-to-Container Communication**: Done by pods and localhost communications.

- **Pod-to-Pod Communication**: We will be mostly discussing this part in this chapter.

- **Pod-to-Service Communication**: Done by services, covered in Chapter 6.

- **External-to-Service Communication**: This is also done by services.

Figure 16-1 shows a high-level overview of different types of communications within a Kubernetes cluster.

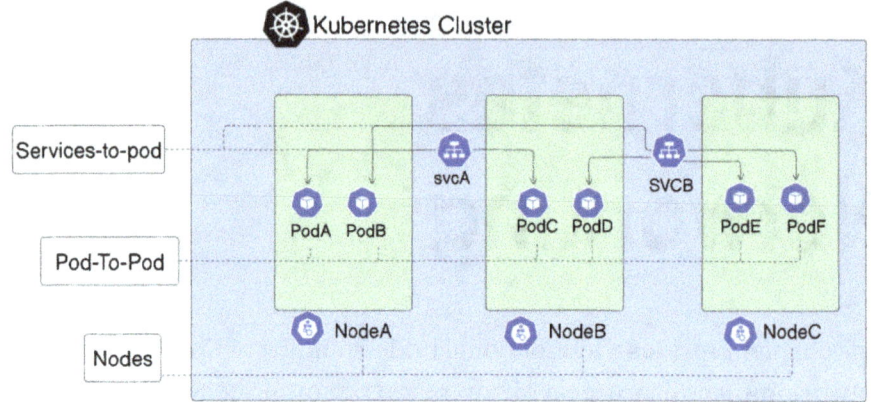

Figure 16-1. Communication within a Kubernetes cluster

Pod Connectivity

In Kubernetes, multiple applications share multiple machines (nodes); however, we could come across the issue where multiple applications are trying to fight for the same port. Each of the control plane components runs on a dedicated predefined port; however, user workloads do not follow any such semantics. It is crucial to have a mechanism that controls the behavior of port allocation and makes sure they don't coincide with each other on a cluster.

To overcome this issue, Kubernetes implements a networking model that gives responsibility to each of the components for the IP address management. Each pod is isolated and gets its own IP address, which allows for secure communication and avoids port conflicts.

- **The Network plugin** is responsible for assigning IP addresses to pods.

- **Kube-API Server** is responsible for assigning IP addresses to Kubelets.

- **Kubelet** (or Cloud Controller Manager in the case of a managed cloud service) is responsible for assigning IP addresses to nodes.

Container Network Interface (CNI)

To implement the networking model, the container runtime on each node uses a Container Network Interface (CNI) plugin to manage the security and networking aspect of the cluster by creating an interval virtual network overlay. Pods within a Kubernetes cluster can communicate with each other using their internal IP addresses.

There are a wide range of CNI plugins available from many different vendors and can be used based on the requirements. For example, CNI plugins such as Flannel do not support network policy implementation; for that, you can use Calico or Cilium.

All the supported CNI plugins can be found here:

https://kubernetes.io/docs/concepts/cluster-administration/addons/#networking-and-network-policy

CNI defines the standard and specifications of how these plugins can be created by making use of the available libraries in the Go source code. It also provides a template for making new plugins and a separate repository containing the reference plugins.

You can check the CNI open source project over here: https://github.com/containernetworking/cni.

CoreDNS

CoreDNS is the default Domain Name System (DNS) management service for Kubernetes. Before Kubernetes version 1.21, kube-dns was the default service, which has now been replaced by CoreDNS.

When you create a service in Kubernetes, CoreDNS is responsible for mapping the IP address to the service hostname so that the service can be accessed using its hostname within the cluster without using the IP address.

CoreDNS runs as a deployment in the kube-system namespace exposed through a service of type clusterIP and named kube-dns.

When you create a new pod in the Kubernetes cluster, CoreDNS creates an entry in the /etc/resolv.conf of that pod that looks something like this:

```
search default.svc.cluster.local svc.cluster.local
cluster.local
nameserver 10.0.0.10
options ndots:5
```

where 10.0.0.10 is the service IP address for the CoreDNS deployment. If you were not using a DNS server such as CoreDNS, you need to add a mapping inside /etc/hosts file of the pod to allow the access from one pod to another. If you are using CoreDNS, you don't need to perform this step.

Troubleshooting DNS Resolution

To debug the DNS resolution in the cluster, you can start by installing the sample pod using the image dnsutils:

```
apiVersion: v1
kind: Pod
```

CHAPTER 16   KUBERNETES NETWORKING

```
metadata:
  name: dnsutils
  namespace: default
spec:
  containers:
  - name: dnsutils
    image:    registry.k8s.io/e2e-test-images/agnhost:2.39
    imagePullPolicy: IfNotPresent
  restartPolicy: Always
```

After applying the manifest, your dnsutils pod should be provisioned inside the default namespace.

Once that pod is running, you can exec nslookup in that pod. If you see something like the following, DNS is working correctly:

```
kubectl exec -i -t dnsutils -- nslookup kubernetes.default

Server:    10.0.0.10
Address 1: 10.0.0.10

Name:      kubernetes.default
Address 1: 10.0.0.1
```

If there are issues with your DNS resolution, you could see the errors as below:

```
Server:    10.0.0.10
Address 1: 10.0.0.10

nslookup: can't resolve 'kubernetes.default'
```

The first step is to check if your DNS pods are running:

```
kubectl get pods -n=kube-system -l k8s-app=kube-dns
```

CHAPTER 16 KUBERNETES NETWORKING

Then look for the errors using the command below:

```
kubectl logs -n=kube-system -l k8s-app=kube-dns
```

Also, verify if the DNS service is up and endpoints are exposed:

```
kubectl get svc -n=kube-system
kubectl get endpoints kube-dns -n=kube-system
```

Verify the CoreDNS configmap for the plugins and if it is forwarding the traffic through /etc/resolv.conf. Alternatively, you can add the log plugin inside the Corefile of configmap to trace all the DNS queries being processed and received:

```
kubectl -n kube-system edit configmap coredns

apiVersion: v1
kind: configmap
metadata:
  name: coredns
  namespace: kube-system
data:
  Corefile: |
    .:53 {
        log  # add this
        errors
        health
        kubernetes cluster.local in-addr.arpa ip6.arpa {
          pods insecure
          upstream
          fallthrough in-addr.arpa ip6.arpa
        }
        prometheus :9153
        forward . /etc/resolv.conf
```

```
        cache 30
        loop
        reload
        loadbalance
}
```

Finally, check the CNI plugin if all the pods are up and healthy.

Ingress in Kubernetes

Ingress helps route HTTP and HTTPS traffic from outside the cluster to the services within the cluster. It works in a similar way to services (NodePort and Load Balancer); however, it adds an additional routing layer on top of the service that does the rule-based routing.

You define the rules inside your Ingress resource; based on the rules, the traffic will be routed to the service inside the cluster.

Let's understand why Ingress is preferred over a Load Balancer service:

> **Cloud Vendor Lock-In**: If you are using a cloud provider such as AWS and create a service of type load balancer, the Cloud Controller Manager (CCM), which is a component of the cloud provider and interacts with your API Server, creates an external load balancer; hence, this approach is not feasible if you are on-premises or using your own data center.

> **Costly Solution**: As you are using a load balancer service, your CCM will provision a load balancer for each of the services that you define in your cluster, making it a costly solution.

CHAPTER 16 KUBERNETES NETWORKING

Security: You need to use the cloud provider's built-in security for the load balancer.

Ingress, as the name suggests, controls the traffic coming inside your application or inbound traffic. To implement Ingress, we need a few resources:

- **Ingress Resource**: A Kubernetes object that defines routing rules

- **Ingress Controller**: The implementation that enforces these rules, such as the `Nginx Ingress controller` that watches your Ingress resource and manages the load balancer

- **Load Balancer**: Created and managed by the Ingress controller based on the Ingress resource YAML

Figure 16-2 shows the lifecycle of Ingress and its dependent resources.

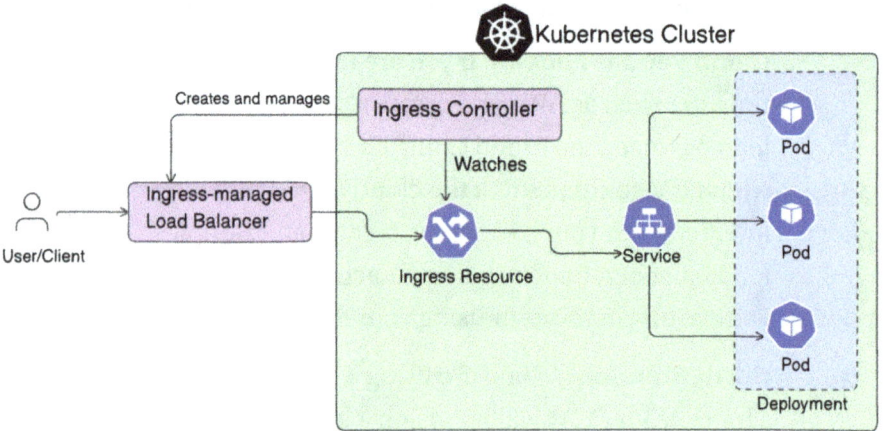

Figure 16-2. Ingress in Kubernetes

Set Up an Ingress

To set up Ingress, you should be creating an Ingress resource, an Ingress controller that watches the Ingress resource, and a Load Balancer that is being created and managed by the Ingress controller.

Ingress Controller Setup

To use an Ingress resource, you should create an Ingress controller such as Nginx that watches your Ingress resource. Using Ingress without the Ingress controller would not work and has no effect.

For example, you can create an Ingress-Nginx controller using the below steps:

https://kubernetes.github.io/ingress-nginx/deploy/

```
helm upgrade --install ingress-nginx ingress-nginx \
  --repo https://kubernetes.github.io/ingress-nginx \
  --namespace ingress-nginx --create-namespace
```

Once the deployment is complete, you should see the Ingress-nginx pods running in the namespace ingress-nginx:

```
kubectl get pods --namespace=ingress-nginx
```

Ingress Resource

An Ingress resource could be created that accepts the incoming traffic from the client and routes it to the backend service(s) based on the defined routing rules. Think of it as a traffic controller that sits at the edge of your Kubernetes cluster, directing incoming requests to the appropriate services based on configured routing rules.

CHAPTER 16   KUBERNETES NETWORKING

Let's understand Ingress with the help of a sample declarative YAML:

```yaml
apiVersion: networking.k8s.io/v1
kind: Ingress
metadata:
  name: hello-world
  annotations:
    nginx.ingress.kubernetes.io/rewrite-target: /
spec:
  ingressClassName: nginx
  rules:
  - host: "example.com"
    http:
      paths:
      - path: /
        pathType: Prefix
        backend:
          service:
            name: hello-world
            port:
              number: 80
```

In the above example, we are creating a resource of type Ingress that is based on the nginx Ingress class, which would have been already created with the Ingress controller Helm chart. If you edit or run a describe on the Ingress controller pod, you find the value of the default ingress class name, such as nginx. This is how the controller will know which resource it has to watch.

The YAML also has a routing rule that says if anyone tries to access the application on the path `example.com/`, redirect the traffic to the service named `hello-world` on port 80.

The annotation nginx.ingress.kubernetes.io/rewrite-target: / will make sure that the incoming requests received on the path (rules→http→paths→path) / will be forwarded to the path defined in the rewrite target. For example, the path contains /web, and the containers have been configured to serve the web page from the path /var/html/www/, so you can create a rewrite rule that forwards the request from /web to /var/html/www inside the container.

You can also use below imperative command for the same:

```
kubectl create ingress hello-world \
  --rule="example.com/=hello-world:80"
```

If you are using a KinD cluster or Kubeadm cluster, the Ingress controller will not create a load balancer resource, and your Ingress will not get an external IP address because this is done by the Cloud Controller Manager, which is a part of managed cloud services such as AKS, EKS, or GKE.

Similarly, we can have our Ingress redirecting the traffic on multiple backend services based on the rules as below:

```
apiVersion: networking.k8s.io/v1
kind: Ingress
metadata:
  name: basic-ingress
  annotations:
    nginx.ingress.kubernetes.io/rewrite-target: /
spec:
ingressClassName: nginx
  rules:
  - http:
      paths:
      - path: /app1
        pathType: Prefix
```

```
      backend:
        service:
          name: app1-service
          port:
            number: 80
    - path: /app2
      pathType: Prefix
      backend:
        service:
          name: app2-service
          port:
            number: 80
```

In this example, the app listening on the /app1 path will be redirected to the app1 service on port 80, and the app listening on the /app2 path will be redirected to the app2 service on port 80 using the nginx ingress class.

Similarly, you can also use Ingress to serve multiple domains using name-based virtual routing.

```
apiVersion: networking.k8s.io/v1
kind: Ingress
metadata:
  name: virtual-host-ingress
spec:
ingressClassName: nginx
  rules:
  - host: foo.example.com
    http:
      paths:
      - path: /
        pathType: Prefix
        backend:
```

```
          service:
            name: foo-service
            port:
              number: 80
    - host: bar.example.com
      http:
        paths:
        - path: /
          pathType: Prefix
          backend:
            service:
              name: bar-service
              port:
                number: 80
```

In this example, the traffic listening on `foo.example.com` on the / path will be redirected to the backend service called `foo-service` on port 80, and the traffic listening on `bar.example.com` will be redirected to the backend service named `bar-service` listening on port 80.

Troubleshooting Common Ingress Issues

We will now look at the most common issues we face related to Kubernetes networking and how to troubleshoot in those scenarios.

Ingress Not Working

```
# Check Ingress status
kubectl get ingress
kubectl describe ingress <ingress-name>

# Verify Ingress Controller pods
kubectl get pods -n ingress-nginx
kubectl logs -n ingress-nginx \
<ingress-controller-pod>
```

Service Connection Issues

```
# Verify service is running
kubectl get svc <service-name>

# Check endpoints
kubectl get endpoints <service-name>
```

Gateway API

The Kubernetes Gateway API represents a significant improvement in how we manage external access to services within our clusters. As a more sophisticated successor to Ingress, it provides enhanced traffic routing capabilities along with dynamic infrastructure provisioning.

The Gateway API has three stable API kinds:

> **GatewayClass**: Defines the type of load balancing implementation and is managed by a controller that implements the class
>
> **Gateway**: Represents the actual load balancer instance that accepts and handles the traffic
>
> **HTTPRoute**: Defines actual routing rules for mapping traffic from a Gateway to the backend network endpoints (services)

GatewayClass

Gateways can be implemented by various controllers, each with distinct configurations. A Gateway must refer to a `GatewayClass` that specifies the controller's name implementing that class.

Below is a sample YAML for `GatewayClass` implementation:

```yaml
apiVersion: gateway.networking.k8s.io/v1
kind: GatewayClass
metadata:
  name: example-gateway-class
spec:
  controllerName: example.com/gateway-controller
```

In this example, a controller that has implemented the Gateway API is configured to manage GatewayClasses with the controller name `example.com/gateway-controller`.

Gateway

A gateway is a front door of your application hosted on Kubernetes that is responsible for receiving the traffic and further filtering, balancing, splitting, and forwarding it to backends such as services. It could act as a cloud load balancer or an in-cluster proxy server.

Here's a sample YAML to implement a Gateway:

```yaml
apiVersion: gateway.networking.k8s.io/v1
kind: Gateway
metadata:
  name: production-gateway
spec:
  gatewayClassName: example-gateway-class
  listeners:
  - name: http
    protocol: HTTP
    port: 80
```

In this example, a Gateway resource has been created to listen for HTTP traffic on port 80. The implementation's controller will be responsible for assigning the address or hostname to the gateway.

HTTPRoute

HTTPRoute specifies the routing rules of HTTP requests from a Gateway listener to the backend services. Rules defined inside the HTTPRoute are configured in the Gateway, and any changes to the rules will result in the reconfiguration of traffic routes in the Gateway.

```
apiVersion: gateway.networking.k8s.io/v1
kind: HTTPRoute
metadata:
  name: example-route
spec:
  parentRefs:
  - name: production-gateway
  hostnames:
  - "www.production.com"
  rules:
  - matches:
    - path:
        type: PathPrefix
        value: /api
    backendRefs:
    - name: api-service
      port: 8080
```

In this example, HTTP traffic originating from the Gateway named production-gateway, which has the Host: header set to www.production.com and a request path of /api, will be directed to the service example-svc on port 8080.

CHAPTER 16 KUBERNETES NETWORKING

Traffic Flow

Figure 16-3 shows the lifecycle of a Gateway resource and its dependent resources in Kubernetes.

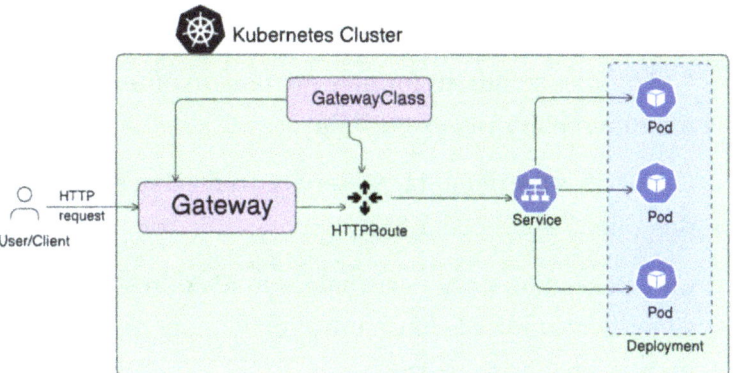

Figure 16-3. *Gateway resource in Kubernetes*

In this example, the client sends an HTTP request to the host `http://www.production.com`. After the DNS resolution happens, the Gateway accepts the incoming request and uses the `Host:header` to match the configuration from the Gateway and attached `HTTPRoute`. The request will then be forwarded to one or more backend pods through the service.

Summary

- Kubernetes networking enables communication across various layers, such as container-to-container, pod-to-pod, pod-to-service, and external-to-service.

- Key components responsible for IP allocation: **Kube-API Server**, which assigns IPs to services; **Kubelet/Cloud Controller Manager**, which assigns IPs to nodes; and **CNI Plugin**, which manages IP allocation for pods.

- CNI plugins facilitate secure communication between pods using an internal virtual network.

- Various CNI plugins (e.g., Flannel, Calico, Cilium) are available, each catering to different network and security needs.

- CNI defines standards for network plugins, ensuring interoperability and extensibility.

- CoreDNS is the default DNS service (replacing kube-dns since Kubernetes 1.21).

- CoreDNS maps service hostnames to IP addresses, simplifying internal communication without needing manual /etc/hosts entries.

- Ingress manages HTTP/HTTPS traffic routing from external clients to services within the cluster.

- Preferred over Load Balancer services due to less dependency on cloud providers, cost efficiency by eliminating the need for multiple external Load Balancer resources, and high security and customizability with routing rules and SSL/TLS termination.

- Ingress resources define routing rules; Ingress controllers (e.g., Nginx) enforce them.

- Ingress requires both an Ingress resource (defines routing rules) and an Ingress controller (enforces these rules).

- The **Kubernetes Gateway API** represents a significant evolution in managing external traffic to cluster services. Unlike its predecessor Ingress, the Gateway

API offers a more improved and flexible approach to traffic routing with enhanced control over infrastructure provisioning.

- The Gateway API architecture consists of three stable components: GatewayClass, Gateway, and HTTPRoute.

- GatewayClass acts as the blueprint for load balancer implementations, similar to how StorageClass defines storage implementations. Gateway functions as the actual load balancer instance, managing incoming traffic, while HTTPRoute defines the specific rules for routing traffic from the Gateway to backend services.

- The typical traffic flow through the Gateway API follows a logical progression where an external client makes a request, DNS resolves to the Gateway's address, the Gateway accepts and processes the incoming request based on HTTPRoute rules, and finally the traffic reaches the backend services and pods.

- The Gateway API provides a more structured approach to traffic management compared to Ingress. Configuration changes in HTTPRoute automatically update Gateway routing rules, and the API supports complex routing scenarios while maintaining simplicity in basic configurations.

CHAPTER 17

Operators and Custom Resources

In Kubernetes, there are out-of-the-box resources and objects available, such as pod, deployment, configmap, secrets, and many more; however, Kubernetes gives the ability to extend the Kubernetes API and create a new resource type other than what is available. Why would you want to create a new resource type? If you have a use case that has not been covered by any of the existing resource types, you can create a new resource as per your specific requirements. For instance, you need to implement GitOps within Kubernetes; in such cases, you can create your own controller.

To extend the Kubernetes API, we have three main objects:

> **CRD (Custom Resource Definition)**: Defining a new type of API to Kubernetes. It's a template that enforces what all fields are supported for the resource and its format.
>
> **CR (Custom Resource)**: Kubernetes validates a CR against the CRD to create your resource and creates the resource in Kubernetes if everything is good.
>
> **Custom Controller**: To manage the lifecycle of custom resource.

CHAPTER 17 OPERATORS AND CUSTOM RESOURCES

When you create a new deployment, Kubernetes validates your YAML or manifest with the resource definition of deployment, whether you have used the supported fields in the correct format or not. Similarly, in the case of CR, Kubernetes will match your manifest with the CRD to validate the YAML with the template.

Figure 17-1 shows the lifecycle of custom resource in Kubernetes along with its custom controller.

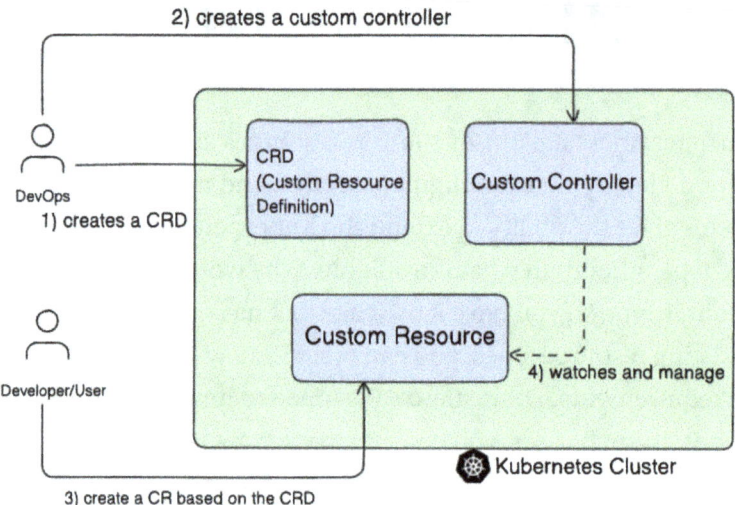

Figure 17-1. *Customer controller, custom resource, and custom resource definition in Kubernetes*

A Kubernetes administrator or a DevOps engineer creates a custom resource definition to implement a custom resource. Then they implement a custom controller that watches the specific custom resource. When a user creates a custom resource, it is being validated against the CRD and being watched by a custom controller to perform certain actions and to manage the lifecycle of the CR.

Custom controllers can be created in any of the supported languages, such as Go, Python, or Java; however, Go is preferred.

Examples of such popular controllers are Prometheus, Crossplane, Fluentd, Istio, ArgoCD, and many more.

CHAPTER 17   OPERATORS AND CUSTOM RESOURCES

Demo Creating Custom Resources

We can follow the below sample repository to implement a simple controller for watching Foo resources as defined with a CRD:

```
# Clone the sample repo
git clone https://github.com/kubernetes/sample-controller
cd sample-controller

# build the sample-controller from the source code
go build -o sample-controller .
./sample-controller -kubeconfig=$HOME/.kube/config

# create a CustomResourceDefinition
kubectl create -f artifacts/examples/crd-status-subresource.yaml

# create a custom resource of type Foo
kubectl create -f artifacts/examples/example-foo.yaml

# check deployments created through the custom resource
kubectl get deployments

# check the resources
kubectl get crd
kubectl get cr
```

Here's a sample workload for the custom resource of type Foo:

```
apiVersion: samplecontroller.k8s.io/v1alpha1
kind: Foo
metadata:
  name: example-foo
spec:
  deploymentName: example-foo
  replicas: 1
```

Operators

In the previous chapter, we have learned how a custom controller manages a Kubernetes custom resource's lifecycle. A Kubernetes operator is used to bundle, package, and manage your custom controllers.

For example, if you are creating a custom controller for Prometheus, a Prometheus operator is used to package the Prometheus custom controller along with its CRs and CRDs and to manage it. When a user tries to perform the Prometheus installation, they can do it via its YAML manifest or Helm chart or even through an operator.

Figure 17-2 shows how an operator works in Kubernetes.

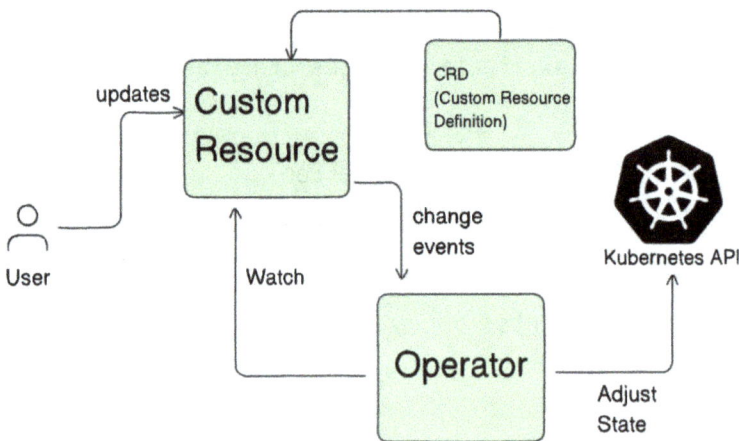

Figure 17-2. Operator in Kubernetes

Operator Features

Installation and Abstraction: A Kubernetes operator enables us to treat the application as a single object bundle exposing only the necessary adjustments instead of various Kubernetes objects that are managed separately.

Reconciliation: In the previous chapter, we have already seen the Helm chart, which contains templates, charts, values, YAML, etc., to install software packages such as Prometheus. However, it doesn't provide the mechanism for reconciliation, which means someone who has access to the cluster can update the deployment manifest and apply the changes to the cluster without modifying the Helm chart or values inside it. If you are using an operator, it has a reconciliation logic that continuously watches the live objects and makes sure it matches the state as created by the operator by automatically scaling, updating, or even restarting the application.

Automation: A Kubernetes operator can be used to automate complex tasks that are not handled by Kubernetes itself.

Easy to Migrate: Just like Helm charts, operators can be easily installed, managed, and transported from one environment to another.

Different Ways to Write an Operator

Kubernetes operators can be written in several ways, each catering to different levels of complexity and developer experience. The Go-based operator is the most powerful and flexible option, offering fine-grained control and deep integration with the Kubernetes API—making it the preferred choice for production-grade operators. The Ansible-based operator allows you to leverage existing Ansible playbooks, making it ideal for those with automation experience but limited programming background. The Helm-based operator uses Helm charts to manage application lifecycles, providing the fastest and simplest way to get started, especially for stateless or templated applications.

Admission Controller

An admission controller is a process running in the Kubernetes cluster that intercepts the API requests sent to the API Server before they are persistent in the ETCD but after the request is authenticated and authorized.

Figure 17-3 shows how an admission controller works in Kubernetes.

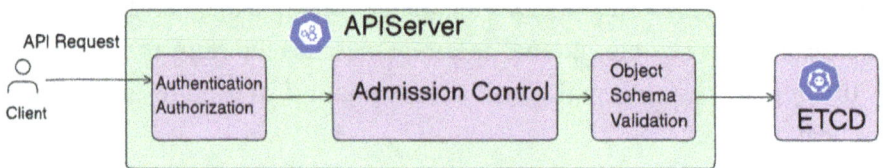

Figure 17-3. *Admission controller in Kubernetes*

An admission control can be of type validating (only validates and accepts/denies the request to the API Server), mutating (makes changes to the object), or both.

In Kubernetes 1.32, the following admission plugins are enabled by default: CertificateApproval, CertificateSigning, CertificateSubjectRestriction, DefaultIngressClass, DefaultStorageClass, DefaultTolerationSeconds, LimitRanger, MutatingAdmissionWebhook, NamespaceLifecycle, PersistentVolumeClaimResize, PodSecurity, Priority, ResourceQuota, RuntimeClass, ServiceAccount, StorageObjectInUseProtection, TaintNodesByCondition, ValidatingAdmissionPolicy, ValidatingAdmissionWebhook.

Admission Webhooks (Dynamic Admission Controllers)

Admission webhooks are HTTP callbacks that receive admission requests and perform actions on them. Webhooks can be easily called via an endpoint or a service reference.

CHAPTER 17 OPERATORS AND CUSTOM RESOURCES

Admission controllers are used to further restrict and manage what objects are submitted to the Kubernetes control plane. Any object submitted to the API Server goes through multiple admission controller phases.

There are two types of admission webhook controllers:

- Mutating admission controller
- Validating admission controller

Mutating Admission Controller: Mutates object submissions before they are validated by the validating admission controller and before they exist in the cluster. It can modify the objects sent to the API Server to enforce certain rules. After the object modifications (mutations) are complete, validating webhooks are invoked for further validations.

For example, a mutating webhook could be called to ensure all pods should have a default label called managed-by: terraform and mutates any pods that do have the field defined as per the webhook's config.

Validating Admission Controller: Defines a validation criteria that ensures that the object is valid in the cluster and will either accept or reject requests.

For example, a validating admission controller requires that all resources have explicit requests and limits set before submission to the API Server and rejects the request if that is not the case.

Figure 17-4 shows how admission webhooks work in Kubernetes.

CHAPTER 17 OPERATORS AND CUSTOM RESOURCES

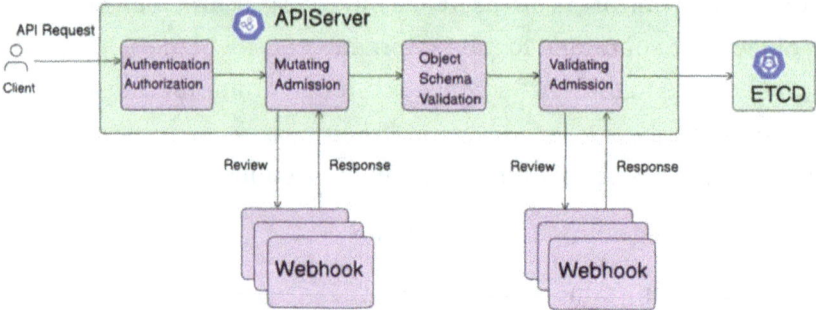

Figure 17-4. *Admission webhooks in Kubernetes*

Here are a few examples where we can use admission webhooks:

- Allowing pulling images only from specific registries
- Label validation
- Adding resource requests/limits
- Sidecar injection
- Replica count enforcement

Here's a sample validation webhook configuration YAML:

```
apiVersion: admissionregistration.k8s.io/v1
kind: ValidatingWebhookConfiguration
metadata:
  name: "pod-policy.example.com"
webhooks:
- name: "pod-policy.example.com"
  rules:
  - apiGroups:   [""]
    apiVersions: ["v1"]
    operations:  ["CREATE"]
    resources:   ["pods"]
    scope:       "Namespaced"
```

```
clientConfig:
  service:
    namespace: "example-namespace"
    name: "example-service"
  caBundle: <CA_BUNDLE>
admissionReviewVersions: ["v1"]
sideEffects: None
timeoutSeconds: 5
```

In the above example, the webhook **pod-policy.example.com**, which is a type of validating webhook, will intercept all the API calls to the API Server that are being issued against the namespace example-namespace and are of type create pods.

For example: `kubectl run nginx --image=nginx`

The webhook (which is a deployment exposed through a service) will receive the request and validate it according to the defined rules. The webhook will then return the response with Allowed or Denied along with the HTTP error code (if any).

Webhook Name and Scope

- **name**: Unique identifier for the webhook
- **scope**: Defines if it applies to namespaced or cluster-wide resources

Rules Section

- **apiGroups**: Which API groups to intercept ("" for core)
- **apiVersions**: API versions to intercept
- **operations**: What operations to intercept (CREATE, UPDATE, DELETE)
- **resources**: Which resources to validate

Client Configuration

- **service**: Kubernetes service that will receive webhook requests
- **caBundle**: CA certificate for TLS verification

Operational Parameters

- **admissionReviewVersions**: Supported versions of the AdmissionReview API
- **sideEffects**: Declares if the webhook has side effects
- **timeoutSeconds**: Maximum time to wait for webhook response

Webook Failure Troubleshooting

A webhook failure can result in object creation failure or result in slow responses from kube-API Server operations like getting, listing, or patching Kubernetes objects. As the failed webhook will keep retrying the calls to the API Server, it will overload the API Server and could cause further issues to the control plane.

A failed webhook should be fixed or deleted to avoid any unforeseen issues.

Common Causes of a Webhook Failure

- No endpoint (pods) available to handle the request.
- Service running in front of the deployment not exposed properly.
- Service referred to in the webhook config does not exist.
- The firewall rule allowing the traffic from the master to the pods on the service's target port is not configured properly.

CHAPTER 17   OPERATORS AND CUSTOM RESOURCES

To fix the issue, verify the workloads using below commands:

```
# Check webhook configuration
kubectl get validatingwebhookconfigurations
kubectl get mutatingwebhookconfigurations
# View webhook details
kubectl describe validatingwebhookconfigurations pod-policy.example.com
# Check webhook service
kubectl get svc example-service -n example-namespace
```

Summary

- Kubernetes allows extending its API through custom resources when built-in features don't meet specific requirements. This extension system consists of three main components:

  - **Custom Resource Definitions (CRDs)**: Templates that define the structure and validation rules for new objects

  - **Custom Resources (CRs)**: Actual instances of resources that conform to CRD specifications

  - **Custom Controllers**: Components that manage the lifecycle of custom resources

- The workflow involves the Kubernetes administrator creating a CRD, implementing a custom controller (preferably in Go), and then users can create CRs that get validated against the CRD specification. Popular examples include Prometheus, Crossplane, and ArgoCD controllers.

CHAPTER 17   OPERATORS AND CUSTOM RESOURCES

- Operators are a way to package and manage custom controllers in Kubernetes.

- Operators continuously monitor resource state and automatically restore desired state if changes occur on the live objects.

- They can handle complex operational tasks beyond basic Kubernetes capabilities.

- Operators can be developed using Go (preferred method), Ansible, or Helm.

- Admission controllers are cluster-level gatekeepers that intercept API requests after authentication but before persistence in ETCD.

- Types of admission controllers: mutating admission controllers and validating admission controllers.

- Mutating admission controllers modify objects before validation.

Example: Automatically adding labels or setting resource limits

- Validating admission controllers enforce validation rules and accept or reject requests based on criteria.

Example: Ensuring all pods have resource limits defined

- Admission webhooks allow for dynamic admission control through HTTP callbacks. Common use cases include image registry restrictions, label validation, resource limit enforcement, sidecar injection, etc.

CHAPTER 17   OPERATORS AND CUSTOM RESOURCES

Services and Networking Review Questions

- Create an Ingress resource that exposes a service on example.com/hello using service port 8080.

- Install an ArgoCD application using the Helm chart by disabling the CRD installation.

- Migrate an existing web application from Ingress to the Gateway API; you should maintain HTTPS access.

PART V

Cluster Architecture, Installation, and Configuration

These topics cover 25% of the exam and focus on the following:

- Managing role-based access control (RBAC)
- Preparing underlying infrastructure for installing a Kubernetes cluster
- Creating and managing Kubernetes clusters using Kubeadm
- Managing a highly available Kubernetes cluster
- Provisioning underlying infrastructure to deploying a Kubernetes cluster
- Performing a version upgrade on a Kubernetes cluster using Kubeadm
- Implementing ETCD backup and restore
- Implementing and configuring a highly available control plane

PART V CLUSTER ARCHITECTURE, INSTALLATION, AND CONFIGURATION

- Using Helm and Kustomize to install cluster components
- Understanding extension interfaces (CNI, CSI, CRI, etc.)
- Understanding CRDs and installing and configuring operators

CHAPTER 18

Cluster Maintenance

Kubernetes cluster maintenance requires various operational tasks to keep the cluster up to date with the security fixes, hardware/software upgrades to get access to the latest features, keeping the cluster healthy to mitigate an ongoing issue, etc. It needs to be performed carefully to avoid any user/business impact. We will look into some of these critical tasks and how to execute them.

Node Maintenance

To perform a maintenance task (kernel upgrade, hardware maintenance, CVE patching, etc.) on a node or a set of nodes, you need to mark the node unschedulable by cordoning the node, which prevents new pods from being scheduled on the node but allows existing pods to continue running. You can use the command

```
kubectl cordon <nodename>
```

It adds a taint to the node that makes it unschedulable.

Drain Nodes

If your maintenance task is disruptive in nature, which could impact the existing workload, such as a node upgrade, then you need to drain the workloads from the node, which safely evicts all the running pods from the node as well as marks it unschedulable. Once that is done, you can safely perform maintenance on the node, such as node upgrades, patching, or even deleting the node (if not required). This activity is known as draining the node, which is equivalent to draining the node and cordoning the node.

```
kubectl drain <nodename> -ignore-daemosets
```

--ignore-daemonset is important; otherwise, the DaemonSet controller will create new pods (the pods were controlled by DaemonSet) as soon as the existing pods are evicted.

Node Uncordon

Once you are done with your maintenance task on the node, you can resume scheduling new pods into the node by uncording the node using the command

```
kubectl uncordon <nodename>
```

Summary

- Kubernetes provides mechanisms for node maintenance without disrupting workloads:
  - **Node Cordon**: Marks a node as unschedulable to prevent new pods from being scheduled while allowing existing pods to continue running.
  - **Drain Nodes**: Safely evicts running pods from a node and marks it unschedulable for disruptive maintenance tasks, such as hardware upgrades or node deletion. Ensures workloads are safely migrated to other nodes before maintenance begins.
  - **Uncordon**: Resumes normal scheduling of new pods on a node after maintenance is complete.

CHAPTER 19

Kubernetes Version Upgrade Using Kubeadm

In this chapter, we will learn the process of upgrading the Kubernetes cluster created with Kubeadm from version 1.31.x to 1.32.x.

Before understanding the upgrade process, let's have a look at some fundamentals of Kubernetes versioning and the supported process.

A Kubernetes version, for example, 1.31.2, consists of a major release version, which is 1; 31 is the minor release that happens almost quarterly, and 2 is the patch set, which happens frequently for bug fixes and minor vulnerability fixes.

Figure 19-1 shows how a Kubernetes version is formed.

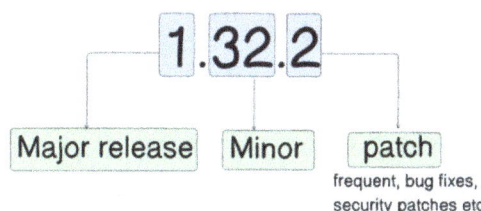

Figure 19-1. Kubernetes version

You can upgrade from one minor version to the next minor version, but you cannot perform the skip version upgrade as it is not supported. For example, you can upgrade from `1.29.x` to `1.30.x`, but you cannot do `1.29.x` to `1.31.x`; in this case, you first have to upgrade from `1.29.x` to `1.30.x` and then from `1.30.x` to `1.31.x`. In short, you can upgrade only one minor version at a time.

Figure 19-2 shows that you cannot perform a skip version upgrade, and it should be done one version at a time.

Figure 19-2. *Kubernetes supported version upgrade process*

Kubernetes Upgrade Process

On a high level, we will follow the below upgrade steps:

- Upgrade the master node.

- Upgrade additional master nodes (if you are using multiple masters).

- Upgrade the worker node.

Note When the master is down, management operations will be paused; however, your existing pods continue to run. For instance, you will not be able to run kubectl commands as your API Server is down; if your pod crashes, a new pod will not be provisioned as your controller manager is down, etc.

Upgrade Master Node

SSH into the master node and run the below command to find the latest 1.32 patch release. It should look like 1.32.x-*, where x is the latest patch.

```
sudo apt update
sudo apt-cache madison kubeadm
```

Upgrade Kubeadm Using the Below Command

```
sudo apt-mark unhold kubeadm && \
sudo apt-get update && sudo apt-get install -y kubeadm='1.32.x-*' && \
sudo apt-mark hold kubeadm
```

Verify the Kubeadm Version

```
kubeadm version
```

Verify the Upgrade Plan

```
sudo kubeadm upgrade plan
```

Run the upgrade command:

```
sudo kubeadm upgrade apply v1.32.x
```

Once the command is completed, you should see a similar message:

```
[upgrade/successful] SUCCESS! Your cluster was upgraded to "v1.32.x". Enjoy!
[upgrade/kubelet] Now that your control plane is upgraded, please proceed with upgrading your kubelets if you haven't already done so.
```

Upgrade CNI Provider Plugin

Depending upon the CNI plugin you are using, you can follow the instructions to upgrade the provider plugin: https://kubernetes.io/docs/concepts/cluster-administration/addons/.

> **Note** This step is not needed for the exam unless explicitly told.

Drain the Node

Drain the node for maintenance by marking it cordoned and evicting the workloads:

```
kubectl drain <node-to-drain> --ignore-daemonsets
```

Upgrade the kubelet and kubectl

```
sudo apt-mark unhold kubelet kubectl && \
sudo apt-get update && sudo apt-get install -y kubelet='1.32.x-x' kubectl='1.30.x-x && \
sudo apt-mark hold kubelet kubectl
```

Restart kubelet

```
sudo systemctl daemon-reload
sudo systemctl restart kubelet
```

Uncordon the Node

```
kubectl uncordon <node-to-uncordon>
```

Verify the Upgrade on Control Plane Node

`kubectl get nodes` should show the upgraded version on the control plane node.

Upgrade Worker Node

Once the control plane node is upgraded, you perform the same tasks on worker nodes as well. Once all the worker nodes are upgraded, you can verify the upgrade version by running

`kubectl get nodes`

All the nodes (control plane and workers) should show the upgraded version `1.32.x-x`.

Summary

- This chapter outlined the process of upgrading a Kubernetes cluster created with Kubeadm from version 1.31.x to 1.32.x (only one minor version at a time). Skipping minor versions is not allowed/supported.

- The upgrade process involves the following high-level steps:

    - **Upgrade the Master Node**: Update Kubeadm, apply the upgrade, and ensure the control plane components are upgraded. Management operations will pause temporarily, but existing pods will continue running.

- **Upgrade Additional Master Nodes**: If using multiple master nodes, repeat the process for each.

- **Upgrade Worker Nodes**: Perform similar steps as for master nodes, ensuring all nodes are updated to the new version.

- The process also includes draining and uncordoning nodes during upgrades to minimize disruption and restarting components like kubelet after updates.

- Once complete, all nodes (control plane and workers) should reflect the upgraded Kubernetes version.

Cluster Architecture, Installation, and Configuration Review Questions

- Perform cluster upgrade from one release to another, for example, 1.30.1 to 1.31.1; upgrade control plane as well as worker nodes.

- Create an additional worker node and join to the master, then drain one of the existing nodes and migrate the workload to the newer node.

PART VI

Troubleshooting

This topic covers 30% of the exam and focuses on the following:

- Evaluating cluster and node logging
- Understanding how to monitor applications
- Managing container stdout and stderr logs
- Troubleshooting application failure
- Troubleshooting cluster component failure
- Troubleshooting networking

CHAPTER 20

Monitoring, Logging, and Alerting

In Chapter 10, we have learned about the `Metrics Server` in Kubernetes. Now we will discuss more on how it works. A Metrics Server represents a critical component in the cluster's monitoring architecture, serving as the foundation for resource metrics collection and exposure.

Monitor Cluster Components

We have `Kubelet` running on each node, acting as the primary node agent that manages containers and maintains communication with the control plane. Working alongside Kubelet is `cAdvisor`, a specialized monitoring daemon that's integrated directly into `Kubelet`. cAdvisor's primary responsibility is to collect and aggregate real-time resource metrics from the container runtime and forward them to Kubelet. Kubelet also receives pod data from the node, such as `CPU` and `memory` details.

The Metrics Server transforms this raw data into a standardized format and exposes it through the `Metrics API`, making it accessible to various Kubernetes components.

The metrics also become available through kubectl commands like `kubectl top node` and `kubectl top pod`, providing administrators with quick insights into resource utilization for monitoring and features like HPA and VPA to work.

Figure 20-1 shows how a Metrics Server works in Kubernetes.

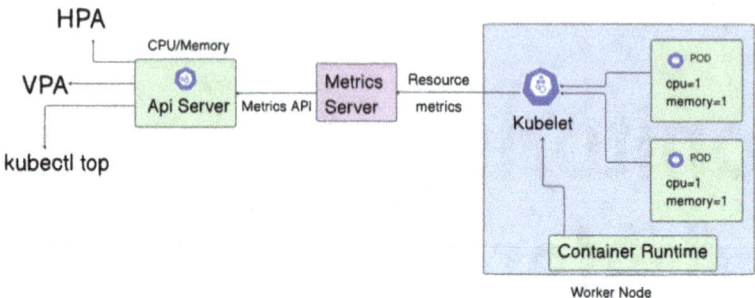

Figure 20-1. Metrics Server in Kubernetes

The main purpose of the Metrics Server is to fetch the resource metrics and node metrics, such as CPU and memory, from the kubelet and expose them in the Kubernetes `API Server` through the `Metrics API` to be used by HPA and VPA. The `metrics-server` calls the `kubelet API` to collect metrics from each node on the endpoint `/metrics/resource`.

Cluster and Node Logging

Logs are generated by all the pods locally on the Kubernetes nodes as `STDOUT` (standard output) and `STDERR` (standard error). Kubernetes comes with limited monitoring and logging capabilities, and we generally use third-party monitoring, logging, and alerting solutions to extend its capabilities.

By default, these logs are not transferred to a third-party monitoring and logging solution such as `Splunk` or `EFK/ELK`; however, as a Kubernetes Admin/DevOps Engineer, we should be well versed with integrating an end-to-end monitoring and logging solution.

CHAPTER 20   MONITORING, LOGGING, AND ALERTING

Debugging Kubernetes Nodes with Crictl

As we discussed in Chapter 2, Containerd is the default container runtime after Kubernetes 1.24, replacing Docker. With that introduction, we can no longer use Docker commands to debug applications and nodes; instead, we use a tool called crictl.

If you are running Kubernetes 1.24+, you should already have crictl installed on your Ubuntu machine, as it comes with the container runtime.

crictl works in a similar fashion to Docker commands with some exceptions. In the Docker runtime, you use the Docker ps command to check all the running containers; with crictl, you use crictl ps.

If you are using Kubernetes 1.24+, Docker commands will not work, so you can also use crictl commands to troubleshoot the issue. This is also helpful in case your API Server is down, meaning the kubectl commands will not work.

> **Note**   In the exam sandbox environment, crictl would also be installed; however, the Docker command wouldn't work.

Let's have a look on some of the important commands:
To list all the pods

```
crictl pods
```

   # To list all the pods with a label

```
crictl pods -label app=nginx
```

   # To list all the images

```
crictl images
```

   # To list images with repository

```
crictl images nginx
```

211

To list all the containers

```
crictl ps -a
```

To list all the running containers

```
crictl ps
```

To execute a command inside a container

```
crictl exec -it <containerid> <command>
```

To get all container logs

```
crictl logs <containerid>
```

To pull an image

```
crictl pull busybox
```

You can read more about crictl debugging using the link below:

https://kubernetes.io/docs/tasks/debug/debug-cluster/crictl/

Summary

- The Metrics Server plays an important role in Kubernetes by collecting and exposing resource metrics through the Metrics API.
- It works with Kubelet, which gathers metrics from the container runtime via cAdvisor.
- The data is collected and aggregated, enabling features like HPA and VPA while providing insights into resource utilization.

CHAPTER 20 MONITORING, LOGGING, AND ALERTING

- Logs in Kubernetes are generated locally on nodes and are limited to STDOUT and STDERR.

- To extend logging and monitoring, third-party solutions like Splunk or ELK/EFK are commonly integrated. These solutions enhance Kubernetes' native capabilities for comprehensive monitoring and alerting.

- For clusters using Containerd as the default runtime (post-Kubernetes 1.24), debugging nodes requires the use of crictl instead of Docker commands.

- crictl enables administrators to manage and troubleshoot containers even if the API Server is down, ensuring operational continuity.

CHAPTER 21

Troubleshooting Application Failure

In this chapter, we'll explore common application deployment issues you might encounter during the CKA exam and in real-world scenarios. We'll cover systematic approaches to understand the issue, common causes, diagnostic steps, and common mitigation steps using kubectl commands and best practices. This list is not exhaustive; however, it contains common application failure scenarios.

ImagePullErrors

ImagePullErrors occur when Kubernetes cannot retrieve the container image from the specified registry. This is one of the most common issues you'll encounter.

Common Causes

- Incorrect image name or tag specified in the manifest file or the kubectl command
- Private registry authentication issues, incorrect credentials, secrets, etc.
- Registry availability problems (server-side issues)

CHAPTER 21   TROUBLESHOOTING APPLICATION FAILURE

Diagnostic Steps

1. Check the pod status:

   ```
   kubectl get pod <pod-name> -n <namespace>
   ```

2. Examine detailed pod information and the latest events:

   ```
   kubectl describe pod <pod-name> -n <namespace>
   ```

Look for events like

```
Failed to pull image "nginx:latestt": rpc error: code = Unknown
desc = Error response from daemon:
manifest for nginx:latestt not found: manifest unknown:
manifest unknown
```

Resolution Examples

1. Fix typos in the image name and make sure that the registry name, image name, and tag are valid and exist:

   Before

   ```
   spec:
     containers:
     - name: nginx
       image: nginx:latestt   # Incorrect
   ```

   After

   ```
   spec:
     containers:
     - name: nginx
       image: nginx:latest   # Correct
   ```

2. Add ImagePullSecrets for private registries and ensure the validity of secret:

```
apiVersion: v1
kind: Pod
metadata:
  name: private-app
spec:
  containers:
  - name: app
    image: private-registry.io/app:v1
    imagePullSecrets:
    - name: regcred
```

CrashLoopBackOff

CrashLoopBackOff indicates that a pod repeatedly starts, crashes, and restarts.

Common Causes

- Application errors
- Invalid configuration
- Resource constraints
- Missing dependencies

Diagnostic Steps

1. Check pod logs:

   ```
   kubectl logs <pod-name> -n <namespace>
   kubectl logs <pod-name> -n <namespace> --previous
   # For previous container instance
   ```

CHAPTER 21   TROUBLESHOOTING APPLICATION FAILURE

2. Check the container startup probe:

   kubectl describe pod <pod-name> -n <namespace>

Resolution Example

```
apiVersion: v1
kind: Pod
metadata:
  name: app-pod
spec:
  containers:
  - name: app
    image: app:v1
    resources:
      requests:
        memory: "64Mi"
        cpu: "250m"
      limits:
        memory: "128Mi"
        cpu: "500m"
    # Add proper readiness/liveness probes
    readinessProbe:
      httpGet:
        path: /healthz
        port: 8080
      initialDelaySeconds: 5
      periodSeconds: 10
```

Pods Stuck in Pending State

Pods in a pending state haven't been scheduled to any node; they could be waiting for something or facing scheduling issues.

CHAPTER 21   TROUBLESHOOTING APPLICATION FAILURE

Common Causes

- Insufficient cluster resources
- Node selector constraints
- PVC binding issues
- Taint/toleration mismatches
- Issues with Kube Scheduler

1. Check pod events:

   ```
   kubectl describe pod <pod-name> -n <namespace>
   ```

> **Note** Logs most likely will not be available as the pod was not scheduled yet.

2. Verify cluster resources:

   ```
   kubectl get nodes
   kubectl describe nodes
   ```

Based on your above findings, you can try fixing the issue.

Resolution Example

```
apiVersion: v1
kind: Pod
metadata:
  name: resource-pod
spec:
  containers:
  - name: app
    image: app:v1
```

```
resources:
  requests:
    memory: "2Gi"  # Reduce if cluster can't accommodate
    cpu: "1"
```

Terminated State

Pods in a terminated state have completed their execution or were stopped.

Common Causes

- Container process completed
- OOMKilled (killed due to out-of-memory issues)
- Pod eviction by controller or gracefully
- Manual deletion

Diagnostic Steps

1. Check termination logs:

   ```
   kubectl logs <pod-name> -n <namespace>
   kubectl logs <pod-name> -n <namespace> --previous
   ```

2. Review pod events:

   ```
   kubectl get events --field-selector involvedObject.kind=pod \ involvedObject.name=<pod-name> -n <nsname>
   ```

3. Look for events like

   ```
   Container was killed due to OOM (Out of Memory). Memory cgroup usage exceeded memory limit.
   ```

CHAPTER 21   TROUBLESHOOTING APPLICATION FAILURE

4. Review memory metrics:

    ```
    kubectl top pod <pod-name> -n <namespace>
    ```

Resolution Example

Adjust memory limits:

```
apiVersion: v1
kind: Pod
metadata:
  name: memory-demo
spec:
  containers:
  - name: memory-demo
    image: app:v1
    resources:
      requests:
        memory: "256Mi"   # Increase based on actual usage
      limits:
        memory: "512Mi"   # Set appropriate limit with headroom
```

For Java applications, set JVM memory limits:

```
apiVersion: v1
kind: Pod
metadata:
  name: java-app
spec:
  containers:
  - name: java-app
    image: java-app:v1
    env:
    - name: JAVA_OPTS
      value: "-Xms256m -Xmx512m"
```

```
  resources:
    requests:
      memory: "768Mi"    # Always set higher than JVM max heap
    limits:
      memory: "1Gi"
```

Service Not Accessible

When services aren't accessible, it's often due to configuration issues.

Diagnostic Steps

1. Verify service configuration:

   ```
   kubectl get svc <service-name> -n <namespace>
   kubectl describe svc <service-name> -n <namespace>
   ```

2. Check endpoints and make sure they are listening to a valid IP/IP range:

   ```
   kubectl get endpoints <service-name> -n <namespace>
   ```

Resolution Example

```
apiVersion: v1
kind: Service
metadata:
  name: app-service
spec
selector:
    app: myapp # Ensure this matches pod labels.
  ports:
- port: 80
    targetPort: 8080
```

CHAPTER 21 TROUBLESHOOTING APPLICATION FAILURE

Connection Refused Between Pods and Services

Connection issues often involve NetworkPolicy configurations.

Diagnostic Steps

1. Verify network policies:

   ```
   kubectl get networkpolicy -n <namespace>
   ```

2. Test connectivity:

   ```
   kubectl exec -it <pod-name> -n <namespace> -- curl <service-name>
   ```

NetworkPolicy Example

```
apiVersion: networking.k8s.io/v1
kind: NetworkPolicy
metadata:
  name: allow-app-traffic
spec:
  podSelector:
    matchLabels:
      app: myapp
  policyTypes:
  - Ingress
  ingress:
  - from:
    - podSelector:
        matchLabels:
          role: frontend
    ports:
    - protocol: TCP
      port: 80
```

CHAPTER 21   TROUBLESHOOTING APPLICATION FAILURE

Service Selector Mismatch

Service selector mismatches prevent proper pod-service binding.

Diagnostic Steps

1. Compare service selectors with pod labels:

   ```
   kubectl get svc <service-name> -n <namespace> -o yaml
   kubectl get pods -n <namespace> --show-labels
   ```

Resolution Example

```
# Service
apiVersion: v1
kind: Service
metadata:
  name: app-service
spec
selector:
    app: myapp
    tier: frontend # Ensure all selectors match pod labels
  ports:
- port: 80
    targetPort: 8080

---

# Pod
apiVersion: v1
kind: Pod
metadata:
  name: app-pod
  labels:
    app: myapp
    tier: frontend # Labels must match service selectors
```

```
spec
containers:
  - name: app
    image: app:v1
```

Summary

1. Systematic Approach

    - Always start with `kubectl get pods`.
    - Use `kubectl describe` for detailed information.
    - Check logs with `kubectl logs`.
    - Review events with `kubectl get events`.

2. Common Commands for Debugging

    ```
    # Get pod status
    kubectl get pods -n <namespace> -o wide

    # Check logs
    kubectl logs <pod-name> -n <namespace>

    # Execute commands in pod
    kubectl exec -it <pod-name> -n <namespace> -- /bin/sh

    # Check service endpoints
    kubectl get endpoints <service-name> -n <namespace>

    # View cluster events
    kubectl get events -n <namespace> --sort-by='.metadata.creationTimestamp'
    ```

3. Debug Container Usage

```
apiVersion: v1
kind: Pod
metadata:
  name: app-debug
spec:
  containers:
  - name: app
    image: app:v1
  # Add debug container
  - name: debug
    image: busybox
    command: ['sleep', '3600']
```

CHAPTER 22

Troubleshooting Control Plane Failure

In this chapter, we will look at how to perform troubleshooting on your control plane from the CKA exam perspective.

API Server Troubleshooting

Suppose you have been given a Kubernetes cluster managed by Kubeadm, and the cluster is in a broken state. The first command you will run is `kubectl get nodes` to check the node status.

If your nodes are in a ready state, that means your API Server and nodes are healthy. If you are getting a `connection refused` error, that means your kubectl is not able to connect to API Server, or API Server is down, or there are some issues with kubeconfig.

To check the API Server status, you can use

`crictl ps | grep api`

Check if the API Server is listed as one of the running containers; if it doesn't exist, that means your API Server is down. You can verify `API Server.yaml` from the `/etc/kubernetes/manifests/` directory.

If the file exists, you can check the errors from a stopped container.

`critical ps -a | grep api`

Now you should see the exited container for API Server.

you should see an error by running the command: `critical logs` on kube-API Server container

You can also check the logs from the default stdout/stderr directory:

/var/log

You can check the API Server manifest and fix it if there are any mistakes; once you do that and if the file is correct, your API Server should be started. Most of the time, error related to API Server should be visible from the API Server container logs.

Now, if you run the `kubectl get nodes`, you should see the result from the kubectl command.

Kubeconfig Troubleshooting

If you are still facing the issue, you can verify your kubeconfig file from ~/.kube/config.

If your kubeconfig is corrupted, you can copy the default kubeconfig file from /etc/kubernetes/admin.conf to ~/.kube/config.

You can also run the command by passing the new kubeconfig to check if it works:

kubectl get nodes -kubeconfig \ /etc/kubernetes/admin.conf

Kube-Scheduler Troubleshooting

The first thing you need to do is run <kubectl describe pod podname> to check the latest events. The events should show some details; if they don't, it makes sense to check the `kube-scheduler`, as this is the component responsible for assigning pods to the node.

CHAPTER 22   TROUBLESHOOTING CONTROL PLANE FAILURE

You can check the logs of the kube-scheduler pod and fix the kube-scheduler pod similar to what we did for the API Server. Once the kube-scheduler pod is healthy, your application pod should be scheduled on a node.

You can verify by running

```
kubectl get pods
```

Kube-Controller Manager Troubleshooting

If you are running a deployment with multiple replicas and you delete one pod, or one of the pods crashed, the deployment controller should be able to spin up a new pod from the deployment template.

In the same way, if you are scaling your deployment and you update the replicas from two to four, two new pods should be created.

If it is not happening, the issue is likely with the `kube controller manager`, as this is the control plane component responsible for managing all the controllers, such as the deployment controller. You can check the controller manager logs and events. After fixing the issue, check if your pods are starting as part of the deployment now.

To check the overall health of your cluster, you can run the command

```
kubectl cluster-info
```

Kubelet Troubleshooting

If you run kubectl get nodes and you see your nodes in a NotReady state, then the issue could be at the node level or at the CNI plugin level.

You can start with verifying your CNI plugin. The CNI plugin installation resides in the directory:

```
/etc/cni/net.d
```

If you are using Calico, you would see a file similar to

`calico-kubeconfig`

You can also check all the running pods and ensure that the pod specific to your CNI plugin is up and running. If you see any pods in a pending/error state, you can debug those using the steps we have followed earlier.

The issue could also be with the Kubelet on your worker node reporting the status as unhealthy. You can start with doing SSH to your worker node:

`ssh ubuntu@worker-node1`

To check the kubelet status, use

`service kubelet status`

or

`systemctl status kubelet`

Ensure the status is running; if it is exited and you don't find much information output of the command, you can try starting the Kubelet using the command

`sudo service kubelet start`

or

`sudo systemctl start kubelet`

If it doesn't start, we can further check kubelet logs using the command

`journalctl -u kubelet`

Go to the latest logs and look for the errors reported by Kubelet. If there are any issues with the Kubelet configuration, they should be reported in the logs.

You can go to the `/var/lib/kubelet` folder and fix the configuration inside the `config.yaml file`. Once done, you can start the Kubelet and make the changes persistent on reboot using the command

```
sudo systemctl daemon-reload
sudo systemctl restart kubelet
```

Summary

- In this chapter, we focused on identifying and resolving issues with Kubernetes control plane components from a Certified Kubernetes Administrator (CKA) exam perspective (most common issues).

- **API Server Troubleshooting**: If the API Server is down, kubectl commands may fail with connection errors. This usually involves checking the kube-API Server container logs, the latest events, and configuration files for errors. Common issues include misconfigurations in the API Server manifest or API Server container itself.

- **Kubeconfig Troubleshooting**: Problems with the kubeconfig file can lead to connection errors. Verifying and replacing corrupted kubeconfig files with default configurations often resolves these issues.

CHAPTER 22   TROUBLESHOOTING CONTROL PLANE FAILURE

- **Kube-Scheduler Troubleshooting**: If pods are not being assigned to nodes, the issue may lie with the kube-scheduler. Checking its logs and resolving configuration errors can restore proper scheduling functionality.

- **Kube-Controller Manager Troubleshooting**: If deployments fail to scale or recover from pod failures, the kube-controller manager may be at fault. Reviewing its logs and addressing any issues ensures proper functioning of controllers like the deployment controller.

- **Kubelet Troubleshooting**: When Kubernetes nodes are in a NotReady state, the issue may arise from the CNI plugin or the Kubelet. To resolve such issues

    - **Verify the CNI Plugin**: Check the plugin configuration files in the /etc/cni/net.d directory and ensure the CNI-related pods are running and debug any in pending or error states.

    - **Inspect the Kubelet**: Confirm the Kubelet service on the worker node is running. If the Kubelet is not running, start it and review its logs for errors. Address any configuration issues in the Kubelet's config.yaml file.

CHAPTER 23

JSONPath

When you interact with a kube-API Server by executing a command such as `kubectl get nodes`, by default it returns a JSON response with a huge amount of information and metadata. Kubectl intercepts that JSON payload and converts it into human-readable format.

Figure 23-1 shows the terminal output of how to check for healthy nodes using kubectl commands.

```
Piyush--->kubectl get nodes
NAME                         STATUS   ROLES           AGE   VERSION
cka-cluster2-control-plane   Ready    control-plane   91s   v1.29.4
cka-cluster2-worker          Ready    <none>          66s   v1.29.4
cka-cluster2-worker2         Ready    <none>          67s   v1.29.4
Piyush--->
```

Figure 23-1. *Health status of the cluster*

If you would like to see the JSON payload, you can update the command as

`kubectl get nodes -o JSON`

There are instances when we have to fetch additional details from the API Server; for that, we use `JSONPATH`, which queries the JSON payload of the kubectl command.

For instance, if we want to retrieve the labels from a pod, we can use the command as

`kubectl get pods -o=jsonpath='{.items[0].metadata.labels}'`

This command will return the label from the pod at the 0th index from the items. Items is a list that holds metadata from multiple pods returned by the command kubectl get pods, and we can specify the pod on which we want to query by specifying its index.

You must be wondering how to check the exact hierarchy of the fields that we have used in JSONPath. Well, we can do that by running the command

```
kubectl get pods -json
```

This will print the JSON equivalent of the query, and we can apply filters as per our requirements, like how we did with labels.

Multiple JSONPath Queries to Fetch Details

Let us look at a few more examples.

To fetch the entire object details, we can use a wildcard character @, so your query will become

```
kubectl get pods -o=jsonpath='{@}'
```

If we want to check the field capacity from all the running pods, we can use this query:

```
kubectl get pods -o=jsonpath="{.items[*]['metadata.name', 'status.capacity']}"
```

In this query, we have used [,] which signifies the union operator as we are combining multiple fields such as metadata.name and status.capacity, and we have used a wildcard [*] which will get all the objects.

We can also iterate through multiple values in a loop by using the format range, end, as below:

```
kubectl get pods -o=jsonpath='{range \ .items[*]}{.metadata.name}{.status.startTime}{end}'
```

We can further improve the readability by adding the \t space and \n newline characters to the query as below:

kubectl get pods -o=jsonpath='{range \ .items[*]}{.metadata.name}{"\t"}{.status.startTime}{"\n"}{end}'

A backslash \ can be used to escape a special character, for example, kubernetes.io:

kubectl get pods \ -o=jsonpath='{.items[0].metadata.labels.kubernetes\.io/hostname}'

To add a filter in the query, you can use ?()., for example, to retrieve the external IPs of all nodes by filtering it with the field status.addresses.type==ExternalIP

kubectl get nodes -o \ jsonpath='{.items[*].status.addresses[?(@.type=="Exte rnalIP")].address}'

JSONPATH Custom Columns

You can further improve the readability by adding the header to the query in a specific format by using custom columns.

Instead of -o=jsonpath, we use -o=custom-columns. For example, if we want to get all the images running in a cluster, we can use the command

kubectl get pods -A \ -o=custom-columns='DATA:spec.containers[*].image'

where DATA is the column name.

Similarly, you can have multiple comma-separated column names as below:

kubectl get pods --namespace default \ --output=custom-columns="NAME:.metadata.name, IMAGE:.spec.containers[*].image"

If you want to apply a filter on a particular field, you can also do that using custom columns. For example, if you like to get the details of all the images except where the image name is registry.k8s.io/busybox:1.28, you can use the command

```
kubectl get pods -A -o=custom-columns='DATA:spec.containers[?(@.image!="registry.k8s.io/busybox:1.28")]image'
```

Sorting the Result

You can also use a built-in sort property to sort the results on a specific field by using --sort-by=<jsonpath_expression>.

```
kubectl get pods --sort-by=.metadata.name
```

In the above command, we sorted the results based on the name of the pods.

Summary

- JSONPath is a query language used in Kubernetes to extract specific information from the JSON payload returned by the kube-API Server.

- By default, commands like kubectl get return a simplified, human-readable format. To access the underlying JSON structure, the -o=json flag can be used.

- JSONPath allows users to query, filter, and format this JSON data effectively.

CHAPTER 23 JSONPATH

- Key features of JSONPath include

  - Querying specific fields within the JSON hierarchy using expressions like {.items[0].metadata.labels}

  - Using wildcards ([*]) to target multiple objects and union operators ([,]) to combine multiple fields

  - Iterating through lists with range loops to format output, enhancing readability with tabs (\t) and newlines (\n)

  - Escaping special characters and applying filters with conditions like ?() to retrieve data meeting specific criteria

- Custom columns (-o=custom-columns) further improve readability by adding headers to output and allowing multiple, comma-separated fields.

- Additionally, sorting results by specific fields can be achieved using the --sort-by flag.

Troubleshooting Review Questions

- SSH to your worker nodes and restart kubelet; check kubelet logs and its related configs.

- Restart the API Server by moving the API Server manifest to a /tmp directory and restoring it back.

- Create a pod and exec into it using crictl, and check its logs and status using crictl.

- SSH into the worker nodes and ensure you are able to run kubectl commands; if you are getting the error, copy the kubeconfig from the master node and try again.

- Write the kubectl command to return all running pods sorted by the creation timestamp.

- Monitor the logs of a pod and look for error-not-found and redirect the message to a file.

APPENDIX A

Tips and Tricks

The following strategies helped me ace the exam multiple times, so I thought I'd share them with you as well.

Prioritize Efficiency

- Tackle the easiest and quickest tasks first. Bookmark the rest for later.
- Then, move on to time-consuming but straightforward tasks like cluster upgrades, node maintenance, role/rolebindings, etc.
- Finally, attempt the complex and time-intensive tasks.

Time-Saving Tips

- Utilize the preconfigured kubectl alias k.
- Leverage bash auto-completion for faster command typing.

APPENDIX A TIPS AND TRICKS

- Brush up on vi editor shortcuts:
  - i: Enter insert mode
  - esc: Exit insert mode
  - :wq!: Save and quit the file
  - :q!: Quit without saving
  - shift +A: Enter insert mode at line end
  - :n: Go to nth line
  - shift +G: Go to end of line
  - d: Delete a character
  - dd: Delete entire line
- **Set Context**: Always use the provided command to set the context before starting each task. It's critical! Remember to set the context, else you will end up performing the task in a different cluster and lose your marks. You can copy the command given on top of each question and paste that in the terminal.
- **Copy Commands**: Click on any command in the question to copy it easily. Click, copy, conquer!
- **Elevated Access**: Use sudo -i (when instructed) for tasks requiring elevated privileges. Superuser mode activated!
- **Read Carefully**: Please make sure you complete all tasks within each question. Read twice, do once!
- **Exiting SSH/sudo**: After SSHing into a node or using sudo—i, use exit to return to the original user. Be cautious, as a terminal session might close otherwise. Exit safely!

- **Prioritize kubectl Commands**: Use imperative kubectl commands whenever possible to save time.

- **Kubernetes Quick Reference Guide**: The kubectl cheat sheet provides a quick reference for commands. You can also use kubectl command --help for specific command details.

    ```
    https://kubernetes.io/docs/reference/kubectl/
    quick-reference/
    ```

APPENDIX B

Sample Questions

As the CKA exam is a complete hands-on exam, make sure you practice the below scenarios (the list is not exhaustive):

1. Check the number of schedulable nodes excluding tainted (NoSchedule) and write the number to a file.
2. Scale the deployment to four replicas.
3. Create a network policy that allows access only from the nginx pod in the dev namespace to the redis pod in the test namespace.
4. Expose the deployment as a NodePort service on port 8080.
5. Monitor the logs of a pod and look for error-not-found and redirect the message to a file.
6. Check for the pods that have the label env=xyz and redirect the pod name with the highest CPU utilization to a file.
7. Create a multi-container pod with the images of Redis and Memcached.
8. Edit a pod and add an init container with a busybox image and a command such as sleep 50.

APPENDIX B   SAMPLE QUESTIONS

9. Given an unhealthy cluster with a worker node in a NotReady state, fix the cluster by SSHing into the worker node. Make sure the changes are permanent.

10. Create a cluster role, cluster rolebinding, and a service account cluster role that allow deployment, service, and DaemonSet to be created in a test namespace.

11. Make the node unschedulable and move the traffic to other healthy nodes.

12. Create a pod and schedule it on node worker01.

13. Create an Ingress resource task and set up path-based routing rules.

14. Create a PV with 1Gi capacity and mode as readWriteOnce and no StorageClass; create a PVC with 500Mi storage and mode as readWriteOnce; it should be bound with the PV. Create a pod that utilizes this PVC and use a mount path of /data.

15. Set up cri-dockerd as the container runtime.

16. Create a new HorizontalPodAutoscaler (HPA) named apache-server in the autoscale namespace. This HPA must target the existing deployment called apache-server in the autoscale namespace. Set the HPA to aim for 50% CPU usage per pod. Configure it to have at least 1 pod and no more than 4 pods. Also, set the downscale stabilization window to 30 seconds.

17. Install and set up a Container Network Interface (CNI) that supports network policy enforcement.

18. Rollback a deployment to a previous revision.

Index

A

ABAC, *see* Attribute-based access control (ABAC)
Access modes, 149–152, 160
Across Namespaces, 61, 63
Admission controller, 188, 189, 194
Admission webhooks (dynamic admission controllers)
　client configuration, 192
　HTTP callbacks, 188
　HTTP error code, 191
　mutating admission controller, 189
　operational parameters, 192
　pod-policy.example.com, 191
　rules section, 191
　validating admission controller, 189, 190
　webhook name and scope, 191
Amazon EC2 servers, 134
Ansible-based operator, 187
API server, 9, 10, 16, 111, 188
APIServer Troubleshooting, 227, 228
Application deployment
　connection refused between pods and services, 223
　CrashLoopBackOff, 217, 218
　ImagePullErrors, 215–217
　Pods, 218–222
　service not accessible, 222
　service selector mismatches, 224, 225
Attribute-based access control (ABAC), 111, 119
Authentication, 109–110, 113–116
Authorization, 110, 111
　ABAC, 111
　AlwaysAllow, 111
　AlwaysDeny, 111
　Node, 111
　RBAC, 111
　webhook, 111
Autoscaling, 87
　cluster autoscaling, 92
　HPA, 88, 89
　Metrics Server, 90
　NPA, 93
　types in Kubernetes, 88
　VPA, 89

B

backoffLimit, 68
Basic Auth, 81

INDEX

C

cAdvisor, 209, 212
Calico networking, 139, 141, 146
CertificateSigningRequest, 114
Certificate signing request (CSR) file, 113
Cloud Controller Manager (CCM), 13, 52
Cluster and node logging, 210
Cluster architecture, 206
Cluster autoscaling, 92, 97
ClusterIP service, 48, 49, 55
Cluster maintenance
   drain nodes, 199, 200
   node maintenance, 199
   node uncordon, 200
ClusterRole, 112, 117
ClusterRoleBinding, 112, 117
Cluster-scoped objects, 57
Cluster-wide resources, 62, 191
CNI, *see* Container Network Interfaces (CNIs)
CNI plugin, 122, 146, 165, 229, 230
ConfigMap generator, 104
Config maps, 79–81, 84
Container management challenge
   container failures, 4
   Kubernetes, addressing solution, 5
   Kubernetes, considerations, 6
   operational challenges, 5
   scale and complexity, 4

Container Network Interfaces (CNIs), 65, 121, 122, 128, 165
Container runtime, 15, 16, 143
Container-to-Container Communication, 163
Controller Manager, 10, 12, 13, 173, 229
Control plane
   APIServer Troubleshooting, 227, 228
   kubeconfig troubleshooting, 228
   kube-controller manager troubleshooting, 229
   kubelet troubleshooting, 229–231
   Kube-Scheduler troubleshooting, 228, 229
Control plane components
   API server, 10
   Cloud Controller Manager, 13
   Controller Manager, 12
   ETCD server, 12
   scheduler, 11
CoreDNS, 166, 168, 180
CrashLoopBackOff, 217, 218
Crictl, 211, 212
CronJob, 68–70
Custom controller, 183
   Prometheus, 186
Custom resource (CR), 183–186
Custom resource definition (CRD), 183–186

INDEX

D

DaemonSet, 65–67, 69
Default namespace, 57–59, 119, 163
Default StorageClass, 157–160
DNS resolution, 166–169
Docker commands, 211
Docker exec, 71, 72
Docker Hub, 15, 100
Docker Registry Secrets, 81, 82
Drain nodes, 199, 200
Dynamic provisioning, 150, 151, 157, 160

E, F

Environment variables, 23, 35, 36, 81, 102
ETCD server, 12
ExternalName service, 55
ExternalName type, 54, 55
External-to-Service Communication, 163

G

Gateway API, 177, 178
    dynamic infrastructure, 176
    GatewayClass, 176, 177
    HTTPRoute, 176, 178
    lifecycle, 179
    traffic flow, 179
GitOps, 183
Go-based operator, 187

H

Health probes, 93, 94, 97
Helm
    charts, 100
    components, 100
    install Prometheus, 99
    vs. Kustomize, 107
    package manager, 99
    sample Helm chart, 100, 101
    values.yaml, 101
Helm-based operator, 187
Horizontal pod autoscaling (HPA), 88–92
Horizontal scaling, 6, 88, 97
Host networking, 163, 164
HPA, *see* Horizontal pod autoscaling (HPA)

I

ImagePullErrors, 215–217
Ingress
    Cloud Vendor Lock-In, 169
    controller, 170
    controller setup, 171
    Costly Solution, 169
    HTTP and HTTPS traffic, 169
    lifecycle, 170
    Load Balancer, 170
    LoadBalancer service, 169
    resource, 170–175
    rule-based routing, 169
    security, 170

INDEX

Ingress (cont.)
   set up, 171
   troubleshooting, 175, 176
Init containers, 32–36, 129

J

Job, 67, 70
JSONPath
   APIServer, 233
   custom columns, 235, 236
   payload, 233
   queries to fetch details, 234, 235

K

KinD cluster, 21, 50, 71, 72, 133
Kubeadm
   configure security groups, 135, 136
   control plane components, 133
   high availability using stacked control plane
      certificate management, 146
      load balancer, 143, 144
      requirements, 142
   Kubernetes installation steps, 134
   ports, Kubernetes components for communication, 135
   set highly available control plane, 142
   set master node, to deploy Kubernetes components, 137–141
   validate installation, 141
   virtual machines, 134
   worker nodes for inbound/outbound connectivity, 136
kubeadm-certs secret, 146
Kubeconfig file, 117, 118, 228, 231
Kubeconfig troubleshooting, 228, 231
Kube-controller manager troubleshooting, 229, 232
Kubectl, 139, 141, 143
   commands, 23, 28, 233
   get nodes, 23, 141, 233
Kubelet, 13, 14, 139, 143
   pod lifecycle management, 13
   troubleshooting, 229–231
Kube-node-lease, 58, 63, 119
Kube-proxy, 14, 15, 66, 136
Kube-public namespace, 58
Kubernetes, 52, 113
   certification creation and approval process, 113–116
   cluster, 19, 24
   installation, on KinD (see Kubeadm)
   multi-node installation, KinD, 22, 23
   node, 8
   pods, 123
   resources, 57
   single-node installation, KinD, 20, 21
   storage, 149–160
   token, 81
   upgrade process, 202

INDEX

Kubernetes architecture
    control plane (*see* Control plane
        components)
    distributed systems principles, 7
    master-worker architecture, 8
    nodes, 8, 9
    structure, 7, 8
    worker node
        components, 13–16

Kubernetes cluster deployment
    architectural diagram, 39
    deployment YAML, 40
    kubectl command, 41, 42
    pod template, 40
    ReplicaSet, 39, 41
    version apps/v1, 39

Kubernetes networking
    CNI, 165
    CoreDNS, 166
    DNS resolution, 166–169
    Gateway API, 176–179
    host networking, 163, 164
    Ingress, 169–176
    pod connectivity, 164, 165

Kubernetes version, 201
    skip version upgrade, 202
    and supported process, 201

Kube-scheduler, 71, 72

Kube-Scheduler Troubleshooting, 228, 229

kube-system namespace, 58

Kustomize, 99, 102
    Base directory, 105
    ConfigMap generator, 104
    and Helm, 102, 107
    kustomization.yaml file, 103
    multiple environments, 105, 106
    top-level fields, 103

L

Labels, 73–76, 83

Legacy controller, *see* Replication Controller

Liveness probes, 93, 95, 96, 98

Load balancer, 47, 52, 55, 94, 143–145

LoadBalancer service, 52, 53, 55

M

Manifest management tools
    Helm (*see* Helm)
    Kustomize (*see* Kustomize)

Manual scheduling, 72, 83

Master node/control plane, 9

Metrics Server, 90–92, 209, 210, 212

Minikube, 20, 24

Monitor cluster components, 209, 210

Multi-container pods, 32–36

Mutating admission controller, 189, 194

N

Namespace management
    argument, 60
    bash-completion package, 59

INDEX

Namespace management (*cont.*)
    FQDN, 60
    hostname, 61
    imperative command, 58
    kubectl command, 59, 60
    namespace-scoped
        resources, 59
    pod, 61
    test scenario, 61
    YAML sample, 58
Namespaces, 62
    creation, 58
    definition, 57
Namespace-scoped
    objects, 57
Namespace-scoped
    resources, 62
NAP, *see* Node auto-
    provisioning (NAP)
Network policies, 121
    allow MySQL pod, 126
    backend pod to access the
        my-sql pod, 123
    Container Network Interface
        (CNI), 122
    Ingress and Egress, 127
    PodSelector, 127
Node affinity, 76–77, 84
Node auto-provisioning
    (NAP), 93, 97
Node maintenance, 199, 200
NodePort service, 49–52, 55
Node uncordon, 200

O

Opaque secrets, 81, 82
Operators
    automation, 187
    easy to migrate, 187
    installation and abstraction, 186
    in Kubernetes, 186
    reconciliation, 187
    written, 187
overlays/dev/kustomization.yaml
    file, 106

P, Q

PersistentVolume (PV), 149, 150
    attributes, 151
    dynamic provisioning, 150
    in Kubernetes, 149
    lifecycle, 150, 151
    static provisioning, 150
PersistentVolumeClaim (PVC),
    149, 150
    access modes, 152
    binding, 151
    demo of provisioning persistent
        storage, 153–155
    dynamic provisioning, 151
    in Kubernetes, 149
    reclaim policies, 152, 153
    request, 151
Pods
    connectivity, 164, 165
    container states, 31

INDEX

definition, 28
deployable units, 27
environment variables, 35
error inspection, 31, 32
Kubernetes cluster, 27
Kubernetes objects creation, 28
    declarative approach, 29, 30
    imperative approach, 28
lifecycle, 30, 31
multiple containers, 32–35
in pending state, 218–220
and services, 223
in terminated state, 220–222
Pod-to-Pod Communication, 163
Pod-to-Service Communication, 163
preferredDuring
    SchedulingIgnoredDuring
    Execution, 76
Prioritize efficiency, 239
Production-grade operators, 187

R

RBAC, see Role-based access control (RBAC)
Readiness probe, 93–95, 97
Reclaim policies, 152, 153, 159
Replicas, 40–42
ReplicaSet, 38, 44
Replication Controller, 37, 38, 44
requiredDuringScheduling
    IgnoredDuring
    Execution, 76

Resource requests and limits, 77, 78, 84
restartPolicy: Never, 68
Role-based access control (RBAC), 111–113, 119, 120
Rolling updates/rollback
    imperative command, 44
    kubectl command, 42
    recreate strategy, 43
    replicas, 43
    revision history, 43
    rollout command, 43
    undo command, 43

S

Scaling, 88
    horizontal scaling, 88
    vertical scaling, 88
Scheduler, 10, 11, 76
Secrets, 81, 82, 84
Selectors, 41, 73, 83
Service account, 110, 112, 118, 119
Service selector mismatches, 224, 225
Sidecar containers, 33, 36
ssh-auth, 81
Startup probe, 93–96, 218
Static pods, 20, 71–72, 83
Static provisioning, 150, 160
STDERR, 210, 213
STDOUT, 210, 213

INDEX

Storage
  default StorageClass, 157–159
  PV, 149, 150
  PVC, 149, 150
  StorageClass, 155–157
StorageClass, 155–157

T

Taints, 74–76, 84
Time-saving, 239–241
TLS client and server, 81
Tolerations, 74, 75, 84
Troubleshooting
  application deployment, 215–226
  control plane, 227–231
  SSH, 237

U

Upgrade master node
  drain the node, 204
  Restart kubelet, 204
  Uncordon the Node, 204
  Upgrade CNI Provider Plugin, 204
  upgraded version on the control plane node, 205
  Upgrade Kubeadm, 203
  Upgrade the kubelet and kubectl, 204
  Upgrade Worker Node, 205
  Verify the Kubeadm Version, 203
  Verify the Upgrade Plan, 203

V

Validating admission controller, 189, 190, 194
Vertical pod autoscaling (VPA), 89, 90, 92
Vertical scaling, 88, 89, 97
Virtualization software, 134, 147
VPA, *see* Vertical pod autoscaling (VPA)
vReclaim Policy, 151

W, X

Webhook failure, 192, 193
Worker node components
  container runtime, 15, 16
  Kubelet, 13, 14
  kube-proxy, 14, 15
Worker nodes, 9, 22, 133, 147, 205, 237

Y, Z

YAML/JSON file, 29

GPSR Compliance

The European Union's (EU) General Product Safety Regulation (GPSR) is a set of rules that requires consumer products to be safe and our obligations to ensure this.

If you have any concerns about our products, you can contact us on

ProductSafety@springernature.com

In case Publisher is established outside the EU, the EU authorized representative is:

Springer Nature Customer Service Center GmbH
Europaplatz 3
69115 Heidelberg, Germany

www.ingramcontent.com/pod-product-compliance
Lightning Source LLC
LaVergne TN
LVHW010338260326
834688LV00036B/765